D1111223

# HOUR CHICAGO

# HOUR
# CHICAGO

*Twenty-five
Self-guided
60-minute Tours of
Chicago's Great
Architecture and Art*

## ANN SLAVICK

SOMERSET CO. LIBRARY
BRIDGEWATER, N.J. 08807

*Ivan R. Dee · Chicago*

HOUR CHICAGO. Copyright © 2008 by Ann Slavick. All rights reserved, including the right to reproduce this book or portions thereof in any form. For information, address: Ivan R. Dee, Publisher, 1332 North Halsted Street, Chicago 60622. Manufactured in the United States of America and printed on acid-free paper.

The author and publisher express their gratitude to the sources listed on pages 251–253 (which form a part of this copyright page) for permission to reprint the illustrations in this book.

www.ivanrdee.com

Library of Congress Cataloging-in-Publication Data:
Slavick, Ann.
    Hour Chicago : twenty-five self-guided 60-minute tours of
  Chicago's great architecture and art / Ann Slavick.
      p. cm.
    Includes index.
    ISBN-13: 978-1-56663-743-5 (paper)
    ISBN-10: 1-56663-743-0 (paper)
    1. Architecture—Illinois—Chicago—Tours. 2. Art—Illinois—
  Chicago—Tours. 3. Chicago (Ill.)—Buildings, structures, etc.—
  Tours. 4. Chicago (Ill.)—Tours. I. Title.
  NA735.C4S58 2008
  720.9773'11—dc22          2007051967

# Preface

*Hour Chicago* is a compact introduction to the visual culture of Chicago. The visual arts in this great city—architecture, painting, photography, printmaking, and sculpture—make Chicago special. This book consists of a wide variety of hour-long trips, inviting you to choose those that interest you. Each tour arms you with information about the aesthetic and historical importance of the buildings and other works of art chosen to represent Chicago culture.

This compilation of short tours includes maps, photographs of many of the buildings and artwork you'll see, and directions to get you from one place to another, including sites outside the downtown (or Loop) and Near North areas of Chicago.

At the back of the book, for reference, you'll find an abbreviated history of architectural and art styles along with a glossary of terms. When a word appears in SMALL CAPS in a tour, refer to the Abbreviated Guide (beginning on page 237). When a word or phrase is *italicized*, it will be defined in the Glossary (beginning on page 245). Words in **bold face** are the names of buildings or works of art that you'll see on the tours.

Chicago is so rich in architecture and art that it would be almost impossible to cover everything of interest in the city.

At the end of the book you'll find a list of interesting places not discussed in the 25 tours. All the tours take place in Chicago, but interesting architecture and art may be found in many Chicago suburbs. For readers interested in traveling outside the city, phone numbers for contacting several suburbs are also included at the end of the book.

The history and individualism of Chicago architecture and its art collections are known internationally. *Hour Chicago* will guide you to some of the best resources available in the city. When you are not touring, the book can serve as a general reference guide to art and artists, architects and architecture.

It is not difficult to find your way around Chicago if you understand the logical grid system implemented in the city in 1909. State Street and Madison Street are at the center of the city: everything goes east and west from State Street, and north and south from Madison Street. Even-numbered addresses appear on the north and west sides of the streets while odd numbers appear on the south and east sides. Chicagoans often find it helpful to use Lake Michigan, at the eastern edge of the city, as a starting point in their travels. Bus stops are clearly marked, subway stations appear along State Street and Dearborn Street in the downtown area, and stairways leading to elevated stations are hard to miss. Chicago's mass-transportation system is quite efficient and wide-ranging. (In the maps accompanying the tours, subway and elevated stations in the downtown area are marked with a ❸ symbol.)

*Hour Chicago* will be valuable to the general reader as well as to the reader who has a history of engagement with the arts, inviting you to choose one, several, or eventually all the tours offered. The breadth and depth of Chicago's art and architecture offers something for everyone and invites you to take part in a Chicago adventure!

# Acknowledgments

Thanks to Chicago for being so fascinating.

Thanks to Joan Friedman, upon whose idea this book is based. Dean Berry for all his excitement and encouragement while I was writing this book. Unfortunately he didn't live to see the final publication.

Charmaine Stilinovich for sharing her expert knowledge of writing. Lilly Ghahremani, whose help and advice was invaluable.

Kara Loring of the Museum of Contemporary Art; Lisa Dorin, Erin Hogan, Adrienne Jeske, and Aimee Marshall of the Art Institute of Chicago; Christina Jimenez of the National Museum of Mexican Art; C. J. Lind of the Smart Museum of Art; Gillian Powers of the Arts Club of Chicago; the Richard Gray Gallery; Chris Roberts of the National Vietnam Veterans Art Museum; Ann Belletaire of the Second Presbyterian Church; Dan Roush of Vinci-Hamp Architects; Gabby Weems of the Regional Transportation Authority; Laurie Domenico of the Arthur Freed Company; Mark Igleski of McGuire Igleski Associates; Patrick Bunetta, Sam and Lenore Darin, Elissa and Jeff Feldman, Howard Friedman, Sunny Gold, Ron Gordon, Elise Kapnick, Connie Kieffer, Mary Kostelny, Debbie and Peter Leeb, Leo Leventhal, Colin

Reeves, Nancy Robertson, Hank Stein, John Vranicar, Lawrence Ware, and John Warsaw.

Special thanks to Ivan Dee for having the faith to publish this book and for his wise advice, and to Stephanie Frerich, managing editor at Ivan R. Dee, for her careful editing and her cheerful help in answering my endless questions.

A. S.

*Chicago*
*March 2008*

# Contents

# HOUR CHICAGO

# Introduction

Chicago is like a wonderful grape: if you hold it up to the light it looks transparent, but it isn't. It's dense and often mysterious. When you peel off the slightly tough outer skin you come to the meaty texture.

Chicago is attractive for many interests: the lowdown and funky as well as the grandest cultural delights. Its many contrasts and treasures are as diverse as the large, important, glowing collection of IMPRESSIONIST painting at the **Art Institute** and the beer-drinking, Cubs-cheering bleacher bums at Wrigley Field. The history of Chicago recalls the notorious Al Capone, the stockyards and meatpacking companies that made the city "Hog Butcher for the World," and much of the finest architecture of the 19th and 20th centuries. It's a city with wonderful parks and a sweeping, expansive lakefront that rims the entire eastern edge of the city and its North Shore suburbs. Chicago also boasts cutting-edge theater, the world-renowned Chicago Symphony Orchestra, the outstanding Lyric Opera Company, and great museums, including the Art Institute, the **Museum of Contemporary Art**, the **National Museum of Mexican Art**, the **Oriental Institute**, and the **Smart Museum of Art**.

Many Chicago residents have spent a lifetime tasting what Chicago has to offer, but if you have only an afternoon or even just one hour to explore this great and amazingly friendly city, *Hour Chicago* will help you take a first sensuous bite of the city. Here you will find tours of architecture, art, and a combination of both.

Chicago's architectural heritage began with the Great Chicago Fire of 1871. The blaze caused a loss of more than 300 lives and 17,450 properties. Within 36 hours, 3.5 square miles of Chicago were destroyed. Despite this tragedy and the overwhelming task of rebuilding, the fire afforded Chicagoans the opportunity to reimagine their city.

Before the fire Chicago was regarded by New York elite as the "second city." The label was a source of considerable irritation to Chicago movers and shakers, who constantly fought the stereotype. Although at a terrible price, the chance suddenly arose to make a new Chicago that would be second to none. Architects and engineers from Chicago and around the world helped redesign and rebuild the city, including Louis Sullivan, Dankmar Adler, William Le Baron Jenney, and Henry Hobson Richardson. Their combined genius created a new, spectacular city on the plains. They wanted a city that psychologically would capture the power and humanistic qualities of ancient ROMAN architecture, consequently equating Chicago's successes with those of early Rome.

Chicago after the fire is the result of those architects and engineers whose planning and finished works continue to live on. Their legacy, and the works of those who have followed in their footsteps, have blessed Chicago with the greatest and most interesting architecture in the United States, if not the world. While Chicago developers and politicians sometimes seem to take giant architectural steps backward, Chicago remains the museum of 20th-century architecture.

William Le Baron Jenney invented the skyscraper in 1885 with the now defunct **Home Insurance Building** in Chicago. Skyscrapers, by moving up rather than out over increasingly expensive downtown land, solved the problem of having enough space to house a rapidly growing workforce.

An additional bonus of moving upward was that owners of these tall buildings were able to collect more rents from the land they owned. Architects used a new kind of construction, an iron *skeleton* (first seen in Paris with the Eiffel Tower), to support the building. The use of these metal bones eliminated the need for heavy, *weight-bearing* masonry and allowed for more windows and light. Builders used tubular concrete caissons, sunk 55 feet into the bedrock, to create a *floating foundation* that effectively overcame Chicago's location on muddy, sandy, shifting earth (the bottom of what had been a lake). The wide *Chicago window* evolved, allowing the maximum amount of light to enter the building in an often overcast city. Later the graceful work of Louis Sullivan led the way for the PRAIRIE houses of Frank Lloyd Wright. In 1909 the influential architect Daniel Burnham laid out a comprehensive city plan which is responsible for the beauty of Chicago's lakefront and the wonderful network of parks that belong to the people of Chicago. The plan for the lakefront and parks remains in effect to this day (with a few exceptions such as **Lake Point Tower**).

With this book you will learn—an hour at a time—about the important buildings and significant art that have put Chicago on the map.

First, some elements to look for in architecture:

(1) Cohesiveness: do all sides of the building complement one another and work as a unit?

(2) As the building rises, look for a beginning (*base*), a middle (*shaft*), and a top (*capital*), just as an Egyptian or GREEK *column* has a *base*, *shaft*, and *capital*. This organizational device is known as *ABA*: *A* = *base*, *B* = *shaft*, *A* = *capital*.

(3) Is there exterior decoration, and does it have a relationship to the rest of the building? Is the decoration integral to the design and materials of the building?

(4) Look at the placement, proportions, and spacing of the windows—do they create a rhythm that is pleasing?

(5) Is the entrance welcoming? Slightly elusive? Bold? What does it say about the overall structure?

(6) What do the building materials convey? Are they rough, smooth, elegant, or do they look tough? The answers to each of these questions tell what the building is supposed to convey to us psychologically.

Great art is about the world: beautiful and orderly, ugly and confused, or a little of both. Artists use line, shape, space, value, color, rhythm, balance, movement, and proportion to convey their message. When viewing a work of art, keep these questions in mind:

(1) How do the elements and principles employed by the artist reveal what he intends to communicate?

(2) Is the work unified, and does it impart a sense of being resolved rather than scattered in its message? (A work of art may appear chaotic, but if chaos is what the artist means to say, the art is successful.)

(3) Does the work speak of the artist's era—socially, philosophically, religiously, economically?

(4) Does the art elicit a response in you, positive or negative?

With these questions in mind, and the tools in the Architecture History and Art History guide, and the Glossary, all at the end of this book, you are now ready to choose a tour.

# TOUR 1

## Early Chicago Architecture:
## Prairie Avenue District

To get to this tour by bus, take the #3 King Dr.
bus, the #4 Express bus, or the #1 Indiana bus
going south. You can board these buses on
Michigan Ave. and take them to E. 18th St. and
S. Michigan Ave. Walk two blocks east to S.
Prairie Ave.

**TOUR 1**

North ↑

ON TOUR

1 Glessner House
2 Kimball House
3 Widow Clarke House
4 Marshall Field House
5 Second Presbyterian Church

This tour takes you to an older neighborhood in Chicago, the Prairie Ave. District in the South Loop, where the very wealthy lived in the late 19th and early 20th centuries. Only a few mansions remain today, but they are well worth visiting.

Starting at 1800 S. Prairie Ave., several 19th-century homes have been restored on a museumlike street that is blocked off from traffic. The **Glessner House**, at 1800 S. Prairie Ave., was designed and built for the Glessner family in 1887 by the famous Boston architect Henry Hobson Richardson. Its design echoes two sides of Chicago society at the time: rugged individualism and elegance for the newly rich who craved refined polish. The windows facing the street are high, designed to afford the family privacy. The main rooms have larger windows but face a private courtyard. The interiors have been restored to their original design and décor with beautiful wood paneling. The Glessner House is a massive stone building reminiscent of a fifteenth-century ITALIAN RENAISSANCE palazzo. Like the Renaissance palaces, this home takes its character from the humanistic concept of the ROMAN

The Glessner House, built in 1887 by Henry Hobson Richardson.

Coliseum as translated by Renaissance architects. It is built of heavy, solid-looking masonry. The stone is rougher (more detailed) at the base, growing smoother, lighter, and less detailed as it moves up the building. The levels are articulated, thus creating the same humanistic response as the *columns* and articulated floor levels of the Coliseum. Like buildings in the Renaissance, the Glessner House is built up to the street, favoring a fortresslike appearance that discourages thieves who wish to "share the wealth" of the people who could afford the palazzi of the RENAISSANCE or the mansions of wealthy Chicagoans.

If you have only an hour, check out the exterior of the houses. The **Kimball House**, 1801 S. Prairie, designed by Solon Spencer Beman in 1872, is directly across the street from the Glessner House, and the **Widow Clarke House** is located at 1855 S. Indiana Ave. The Kimball House is a CHATEAU-STYLE mansion with wonderful plaster *reliefs* and oak woodwork in the interior. Unfortunately it is no longer open to the public. The Clarke House was built in 1836,

The Widow Clarke House has moved around.

making it the oldest house standing in Chicago, its architect unknown. It was built for a wealthy hardware dealer, Henry Clarke, who died in 1849. It remained home to his widow for many years thereafter. Moved from its original site at E. 16th St. and S. Michigan Ave., the house was then brought to E. 45th St. and S. Wabash Ave., and finally to its current resting place. Built in the GREEK REVIVAL style, the Clarke House has humanistic *Doric columns* across the front of the home. At the south end of the block is the **Marshall Field House**, 1919 S. Prairie Ave., also built by Solon Spencer Beman in 1884. This QUEEN ANNE STYLE home has been redone and changed so considerably that it is difficult to see its original character. It was recently restored and now houses six condominiums.

If you have more than an hour, you might wish to take a tour of the Glessner and Clarke houses. Tours are from Wednesday through Sunday, and are on a first-come-first-served basis. Tours of the Clarke House are at 12 and 2 p.m. Tours of the Glessner House are at 1 and 3 p.m. Tours for both houses cost $15 for general admission and $12 for students and seniors. A tour for one house is $10 for general admission and $9 for students and seniors. For further information and to confirm times, call 312-326-1480.

▶  Be sure to save at least 20 minutes to visit the **Second Presbyterian Church** at 1936 S. Michigan Ave., two blocks west of S. Prairie Ave. Built in 1874 by architect James Renwick and remodeled in 1900 by Howard Van Doren Shaw, the church is constructed in the Greek Revival style with impressive stained-glass windows. Seven of the windows are original Tiffany's. Other stained-glass artists are represented, including Edward Burne-Jones, the English PRE-RAPHAELITE painter who designed several windows that were executed by William Morris. The church offers a map of the windows. The murals are by Chicagoan Frederic Clay Bartlett. This church is one of Chicago's least-known treasures. You can walk in from the entrance on

A Tiffany window at the Second Presbyterian Church.

E. Cullerton St., on the south side of the building. The church is open on Tuesday from 9 a.m. to 3 p.m., Wednesday through Friday 9 a.m. to 5 p.m., and Saturday 9 a.m. to 1 p.m. Call 312-225-4951 if you would like to see the church any other day of the week. There is no entrance fee, but a donation is appreciated. For large groups, call the number listed above and you will be provided with a guide.

# TOUR 2

## Old Chicago: The Manhattan Building and the Monadnock

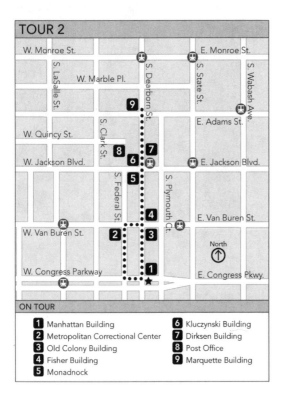

TOUR 2

W. Monroe St.  E. Monroe St.
S. LaSalle St.  W. Marble Pl.  S. Dearborn St.  S. State St.  S. Wabash Ave.

**9**

W. Quincy St.  S. Clark St.  E. Adams St.

W. Jackson Blvd.  **8**  **7**  E. Jackson Blvd.
**6**

S. Federal St.  **5**  S. Plymouth Ct.

**4**  E. Van Buren St.

W. Van Buren St.  **2**  **3**  North ↑

W. Congress Parkway  **1**  E. Congress Pkwy.
★

### ON TOUR

**1** Manhattan Building
**2** Metropolitan Correctional Center
**3** Old Colony Building
**4** Fisher Building
**5** Monadnock

**6** Kluczynski Building
**7** Dirksen Building
**8** Post Office
**9** Marquette Building

Begin at the **Manhattan Building**, 431 S. Dearborn St. (Dearborn St. at Congress Pkwy.), built in 1891 by William Le Baron Jenney, the architect who designed the first skyscraper. This building is the oldest, tallest office building with *skeletal construction* still standing anywhere in the world. Jenney, an engineer as well as an architect, used this new style

The Manhattan Building is the oldest, tallest office building with skeletal construction still standing in the world.

of construction throughout the Manhattan Building, and it became one of the first tall buildings featuring this revolutionary style. It was, for a short time, the tallest building in the world. Built with a *floating foundation*, the Manhattan also has *cantilevered* bay windows that give the entire façade a three-dimensional feel as your eye moves in and out of the spaces created by the bays. The cantilevering relieves some of the pressure the Manhattan exerts on the smaller buildings around it. The Manhattan was renovated from offices to apartments in the 1980s by the Hasbrouk Hunderman firm. It was converted to condominiums in 1997 and recently underwent restoration work.

From here you can see the **Metropolitan Correctional Center** built by Harry Weese and Associates in 1975 at 71 W. Van Buren St. You will recognize this building because it looks like the giant, triangular IBM card that was used in the early days of computers. Here is a true example of form following function: designed as a living and working space for the prisoners, the correctional center, rising 26 floors, has

Form follows function in the design of the
Metropolitan Correctional Center.

floor-to-ceiling windows that are only five inches wide to
prevent escape (though a prisoner once managed to escape
through them) but allow in maximum light. The interior offers privacy and comfort, with the center of each floor serving as a large, multipurpose room. The rooftop serves as an
exercise space. (Precautions had to be taken to prevent "escape" helicopters from landing on the roof.) When the concrete surface of the building needed attention, the work was
not well done, so the sloppily applied protective coating dam-
ages the unity of this creatively conceived, originally smooth-
surfaced building. Pay attention to the inventive use of a pie-
shaped piece of land with a triangular design. Chicago
architect Harry Weese often designed buildings adapted to
smaller, odd-shaped areas.

Note the rounded bays at the corners of the Old Colony Building.

The **Old Colony Building** at 407 S. Dearborn St. was built by William Holabird and Martin Roche in 1894 and was the first building to use *portal arches* as a brace against high winds. The continuous vertical *columns* emphasize height while the horizontal supports make the fairly narrow building appear wider. Notice the rounded bays at the corners of the building. This dramatic device creates interesting shapes and eases pedestrian passage from one street to the other: how much easier to flow with the curve instead of following the sharp angle of most buildings. Art historian Robert Loescher has noted that the rounded corners of some Chicago buildings echo the movement of waves, meant as symbols of Chicago's two bodies of water, Lake Michigan and the Chicago River. Both the lake and the river are an integral part of the aesthetics, economics, and general lifestyle of Chicago.

The open, light, and graceful **Fisher Building**, built in 1896 by the D. H. Burnham Company at 343 S. Dearborn St., tends to be more fanciful in its décor than its neighbors. The *Chicago windows* projecting out in bays bring much light into the inner spaces. Emphasis is placed on the verticality of this steel-framed, masonry-clad building. The décor is NEO-GOTHIC at its best. The exterior *terra-cotta* sculpture features fish, shells, and other sea themes as a reminder of the name of the original owner, Lucius Fisher. This building was in disrepair for some time, but restoration began in 2000. Residents of the new rental apartments enjoy the light and beauty of this grande dame of Chicago architecture.

The **Monadnock** runs along S. Dearborn St. but has its address around the corner at 53 W. Jackson Blvd. The north half was designed by Burnham and Root in 1891; the south end was added by Holabird and Roche in 1893. The newer building masterfully relates to the older building so that our

The Fisher Building uses sea themes in its exterior decoration.

eye translates the two buildings into one. See if you can spot where the old ends and the new begins.

At 16 stories the Monadnock is the largest commercial building using the *weight-bearing* method of construction.

The Monadnock is the largest commercial building with weight-bearing construction.

The base is approximately 15 feet thick to carry the weight of 16 stories and gently tapers upward from the heavy support. The Boston developers of the building wanted to bring a bit of the East Coast to the flatlands of Chicago, so they named the Monadnock for a New England mountain. Originally each entrance was named for a different mountain: Monadnock, Kearsarge, Wachusetts, and Katahdin. The building was refurbished in 1979–1980 by William Donnell. It undergoes continuous renovation to maintain its original splendor.

Without surface décor on the exterior, the Monadnock conveys a sense that it is all business. It curves inward and upward from a wide base and then curves back out at the top *cornice*. The projecting bay windows lighten the appearance of this massive structure. All the offices in the Monadnock have outside windows. This imposing but viewer-friendly building is reminiscent of the massive *columns* of ancient Egypt that, like later GREEK buildings, had a *base*, *shaft*, and *capital*. It has a strong visual relationship to the earlier **Glessner House**. Step into the lobby to see the excellent restoration that brings back images of the late 19th century when the Monadnock was first built.

Take a good look at the **Chicago Federal Center**, across the street from the Monadnock, on S. Dearborn St. between W. Jackson Blvd. and W. Adams St. These three buildings, constructed between 1960 and 1974, are gems of Ludwig Mies van der Rohe's INTERNATIONAL STYLE. Mies's architecture expresses the minimal essence of a building with no extraneous elements, much like its neighbor, the Monadnock. The beauty lies in the elegant proportions, the materials, and the rhythms of the structure. Mies's buildings are minimal sculptures that focus the viewer's attention on the symmetry and grace of the construction, the strength of the building, and how form follows function. The vertical and horizontal lines reflect people's rational, mathematical nature while the diagonal lines formed by the inside lights allude to people's emotional side. Of the three Federal

Alexander Calder's *Flamingo* holds its own amidst the Mies buildings of the Federal Center.

Buildings, two are alike: the **Dirksen Federal Building** at 219 S. Dearborn St. (named after the U.S. senator from Illinois) and the **Kluczynski Federal Building**, across the street at 230 S. Dearborn St. (named after a Chicago congressman). They are majestic towers with human-friendly bases (remember the ROMAN Coliseum) where people can relate to the proportions of the ground floor, see inside to the lobby, and be protected from the elements by an arcade. The *shaft* of each building rises skyward and is topped by a simple *capital*. The third structure of the **Chicago Federal Center** is the low **Post Office** on the plaza that, by its less stupendous size, emphasizes the soaring nature of its companions while maintaining the perfect balance of the space, once again allowing viewers a place to measure themselves against the Post Office's gigantic partners. The buildings are placed on the land to complement each other like three wonderful sculptures. Mies viewed the office building as a "house of work, of organization, of clarity, of economy. . . . Broad, light workspace, unbroken, but articulated according to the organization of the work. Maximum effort with minimum means."

The surrounding plaza gives us an opportunity to breathe, observe the Federal Buildings, and relate them to their neighbors. This triad is finished off with the Alexander Calder *stabile* **Flamingo**. The stabile has a great sense of action and contrasts the straight lines of Mies with the sweeping curves of Calder. It is one of the most effective outdoor art pieces in Chicago because it is large enough and its gesture powerful enough to hold its own with its titanic, geometric partners. It vigorously demonstrates another, more organic way of looking at the world.

The **Marquette Building**, across the street from the Mies complex at 140 S. Dearborn St., was designed by Holabird and Roche in 1893–1895. The building looks like a large grid with repetitive *Chicago windows* alongside strong, projecting horizontals and narrower, less powerful verticals. The doors on Dearborn St. and the lobby are magnificent, decorated with bronze *reliefs* on the outside and glorious *mosaics* in the lobby. The *mosaics* depict scenes from the life and journey of Père Jacques Marquette, and specifically highlight his journey with Louis Jolliet in 1674–1675 to what is now Chicago. The artwork on the door and in the lobby is

Entrance to the Marquette Building and its magnificent lobby.

worth your time; the lobby is easy to access and is open every day.

▶ You have just witnessed Chicago history from the earliest days after the fire through the importance of Mies van der Rohe's INTERNATIONAL STYLE in the 1950s.

# TOUR 3

## The Financial District

**TOUR 3**

W. Madison St.

S. Wells St.

S. LaSalle St.

S. Clark St.

7

S. State St.

W. Monroe St.

6

W. Marble Pl.

North ↑

5 W. Adams St.

S. Dearborn St.

4 W. Quincy St.

2 3 W. Jackson Blvd.

★ 1

W. Van Buren St.

**ON TOUR**

| 1 Chicago Board of Trade | 5 190 S. LaSalle St. |
| 2 Federal Reserve Bank | 6 Inland Steel |
| 3 Bank of America | 7 One S. Dearborn |
| 4 Rookery | |

This tour starts at the **Chicago Board of Trade Building**, 141 W. Jackson Blvd., built by Holabird and Root in 1930, with additions in 1982 by Murphy/Jahn Architects and in 1997 by Fujikawa Johnson and Associates. In 2007 T. Gunny Harboe restored the main lobby. This early skyscraper is at the head or the foot of a financially oriented street, an exclamation point of fiscal authority.

In Chicago, a city with a limited number of authentic and outstanding ART DECO buildings, the Board of Trade is a

The Board of Trade building puts the exclamation point on financially oriented LaSalle Street.

standout. It rises to 45 stories and has a nine-story base housing a fabulous lobby and a six-story commodities trading room. The deep ART DECO *setbacks* of the Jackson Blvd. façade create the impression of a huge throne. This element, plus the continuous vertical *piers* and the windows echoing the tall *piers*, give the building a sense of majesty and elegance.

Nighttime illumination accentuates the building's *setbacks* and creates a glow that encompasses the entire street. Step into the lobby and enjoy the flow of beige and black marble that forms sleek, polished *piers* and other rectilinear forms, rounded at the edges in Art Deco style.

A 32-foot aluminum statue of **Ceres**, the ROMAN goddess of grain (one of the commodities traded on the floor of the exchange), rises from the Board of Trade's pyramid-shaped roof. Created by American sculptor John Storrs, *Ceres* supposedly does not have facial features because Storrs believed no one would ever see facial details at that height. One wonders what he might think if he could see all the buildings looking down at her face now. Accompanying *Ceres* are figures holding sheaves of corn and wheat, created by Illinois artist Alvin Meyer, located on the front façade of the building (look upward to the clock).

In the early 1980s architect Helmut Jahn created an addition at the south end of the original building. The annex, though built of glass and steel, understands, respects, and expresses unity with the earlier structure. Jahn echoes the verticality, setbacks, and the pyramidal roof of the existing limestone edifice. The annex is capped by an octagon-shaped abstract symbol of the commodities trading floor. Jahn's tall, light-filled atrium on the 12th floor of the newer building is a unifying pass-through from old to new. The north wall of the atrium reveals the limestone of the original building. Be sure to view the Jahn addition from the plaza behind the building, and as you walk away from the Jackson Blvd. entrance, turn back and look at the older building from a distance.

It's exciting to watch the traders ply their profession on the trading room floor. This "wild show" of financial trading may be viewed on video at the Visitors Center from 9:30 a.m. to 1:15 p.m. Monday through Friday. Educational or business groups may make reservations to visit the floor by calling 312-435-3590.

As you leave the Board of Trade and walk north on S. LaSalle St., look briefly at two buildings by Graham, Anderson, Probst and White: the **Federal Reserve Bank** at 230 S. LaSalle St., built in 1922, and across the street the **Bank of America**, 231 S. LaSalle St., originally the **Continental Illinois National Bank Building**, built in 1924. Here you see two classic ROMAN structures with massive *columns* and a strong sense of solidity and stability: of being in that place forever in the past and forever in the future. What better image for an institution that houses your money? Note the drawings of the columns at the back of the book to see which of these buildings has *Ionic columns* and which has *Corinthian columns*.

The **Rookery**, 209 S. LaSalle St., was built by Burnham and Root in 1888. The lobby was redesigned in 1907 by a struggling young architect named Frank Lloyd Wright. It is called the Rookery because for many years the building was plagued by masses of pigeons that made the façade their home. The building, originally **Chicago City Hall**, was designed around a huge iron water tank that survived the Chicago Fire. The old city hall that was destroyed by the fire was also called the Rookery because of the "pigeons in residence."

The Rookery's public façades are *weight-bearing* masonry while the alley façade is *skeletal construction* with cast-iron *columns* supporting the floors and walls. This combined method of architecture conformed best to the harsh clay earth beneath the building. The exterior is reminiscent of ITALIAN RENAISSANCE palazzi and also of Chicago's **Glessner House.** It is aggressively built up to the sidewalk with red bricks rising from a red granite base. Heavily *rusticated* stone surrounds the expansive *Roman arch* that forms the main entrance. It has articulated levels, an effective *ABA* design, and a measured rhythm of windows marching across the walls, completing the effect of power as expressed in Italian Renaissance architecture. The *terra-cotta* decoration, a typical Chicago element, was designed by John Root to soften the fortresslike walls.

Step inside the main entrance for a visual treat. The low entry houses wonderful elevators created by William Drummond in 1930. As you continue, you step into the light, airy

The Rookery's central court, designed by Frank Lloyd Wright.

Frank Lloyd Wright–designed central court, a skeletal design capped by skylights. The marble, gold, and *cylindrical* iron staircase, rising majestically to a walkway that circles the mezzanine, is breathtaking.

You're lucky to see it this way. For many years the building was drab and neglected, with the skylight covered and the *mosaic* floors removed. In 1987 the McClier Corporation (now Aecom) shut down the building and began a thoughtful restoration that took four years and brought the entire structure back to its original grandeur. The lobby is open every day but Sunday.

Diagonally across the street, at the northwest corner of LaSalle St. and S. Adams St., is the POSTMODERN building **190 S. LaSalle St.**, built in 1987 by Philip Johnson and John Burgee. Johnson, a former colleague of Mies's and, earlier, a devotee of the INTERNATIONAL STYLE, was one of the artists who declared the less-is-more International Style dead in the 1970s and became a leader of the POSTMODERN movement.

At 190 S. LaSalle St. you can see how Johnson applied historic references by using earlier-20th-century recessed-style windows interspersed with modern glass *curtain wall* windows, gables at the top, and *Roman arches* at the doors. This building has many references to the now defunct Masonic Temple built in 1892 by John Root. Demolished in 1939, it was a 22-story structure at Randolph and State streets. The red granite and Roman arches of 190 S. LaSalle St. echo and respect its neighbor, the historic Rookery. Note how the granite moves from the building onto the sidewalk at the 190 building. 190 S. LaSalle St. was the first building in many years to be built with no retail space at the base.

Entering the quiet lobby, you may have the sense of being in a ROMANESQUE CATHEDRAL, with *vaulted ceilings* completely covered in real gold leaf. The elevators are worth a visit, and at the far north end of the space is a large, wonderful sculpture by English artist Anthony Caro. Entitled **Chicago Fugue**, the shapes of the sculpture refer to musical instruments. (Critics disagree as to whether the proportions of the work are appropriate to the space.) Around the corner at the south end of the lobby is a tapestry by Helena Hemmark depicting the layout of Chicago in the early part of the century.

When you leave 190 S. LaSalle St., head north on LaSalle St. for one block, and go two blocks east on W. Monroe St. to the **Inland Steel Building** at 30 W. Monroe St. Built in 1958 by Skidmore, Owings and Merrill, it was the first building to use steel pilings driven deep into the earth to support this high-rise. On the Dearborn side it moves in and out of space from projecting *column* to recessed *curtain wall* windows, always emphasizing the vertical thrust of the structure that rises to 19 stories and is clad in stainless steel. All service elements and loading docks are in the adjoining 25-floor opaque section at the east end of the office building.

In the lobby you will find a wire sculpture by Richard Lippold called **Radiant One**. The elegant, radiating arms hover over a pool of water. The stainless steel, gold, and copper sculpture is CONSTRUCTIVIST in style. The ethereal work

The Inland Steel Building is clad in stainless steel.

is symmetrical, solidly held in its place but with great fluidity and movement.

Next door and around the corner, **One S. Dearborn St.,** built by DeStefano, Keating and Partners in 2005, becomes a great neighbor to Inland Steel. It refers to the earlier MOD-ERNIST style of architecture in Chicago, creating a glassy exterior that reflects and enhances the older building. It has a fabulous glass-walled entry and a stunning top that houses mechanical equipment. The top is a slice of glass with a cutout featuring frosted glass tilting inward. Night lighting enhances the effect. The ABA solution of this building is effective and even includes a charming little plaza. Peek into the lobby to see the cast glass walls.

▶    This tour points out how important it is for architects, designers, and developers to think of where they are building and what is already at that site. The elements that make for an interesting, well-designed, appealing, and comfortable city are the same as those to be considered in planning a painting, a room, or an outfit for a special occasion. Each component must relate to and respect the other components to be fully effective.

# TOUR 4

## Government Buildings and the Picasso

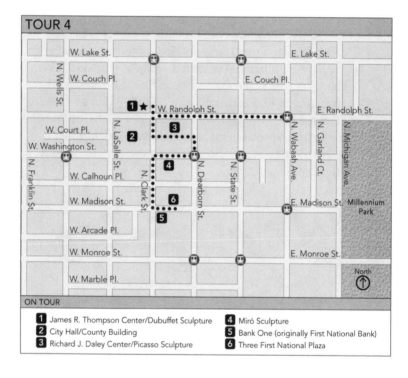

**TOUR 4**

W. Lake St. — E. Lake St.
W. Couch Pl. — E. Couch Pl.
N. Wells St.
**1** ★ W. Randolph St. — E. Randolph St.
W. Court Pl.
**2**   **3**
W. Washington St.
N. Franklin St. — N. LaSalle St. — N. Clark St.
W. Calhoun Pl.   **4**   N. Dearborn St. — N. State St. — N. Wabash Ave. — N. Garland Ct. — N. Michigan Ave.
W. Madison St.   **6**   E. Madison St. Millennium Park
W. Arcade Pl.   **5**
W. Monroe St. — E. Monroe St.
W. Marble Pl.   North ↑

**ON TOUR**

**1** James R. Thompson Center/Dubuffet Sculpture
**2** City Hall/County Building
**3** Richard J. Daley Center/Picasso Sculpture
**4** Miró Sculpture
**5** Bank One (originally First National Bank)
**6** Three First National Plaza

The **James Thompson Center** (or the **State of Illinois Building**) at 100 W. Randolph St., built in 1985 by Murphy/Jahn Architects, has been one of the most controversial buildings in Chicago. Situated between Randolph, Lake, Dearborn, and Clark streets, the rounded shape of the building echoes the domes that top more traditionally designed state buildings. It has a large plaza, which art historian Robert Loescher once noted might be thought of as a space where the state can fend off the enemy: the City of Chicago. (The

The Thompson Center, one of Chicago's most controversial buildings.

skirmishes between Illinois and its largest city are legendary.)
The pinkish-red, blue, and white colors are symbols of the
national colors but aren't effective because they look washed-
out. Speculation is that as the building progressed, funds became problematic, and richer *tones* of red, white, and blue
would have been too expensive. The building rises on Randolph and Dearborn streets like a rounded, glassy spaceship
about to take off, its sloping *piers* reaching skyward. The
LaSalle St. façade flattens as it faces traditional, rectilinear
city architecture.

Inside the building you will encounter a 17-story atrium
ringed by floors that feel like balconies. The effect can be
dizzying. The lobby floor is always busy with various exhibitions, displays, and crowds of people. Originally the offices of
the upper floors were not effectively heated or air-conditioned
because of the tons of glass reflecting the sun or absorbing the
cold. When the building first opened, office workers were
chilled in the winter and fainted from extreme heat in the
summer. In spite of initial reservations and bad press about the

building, Chicagoans have more recently taken to it. Try to see the Illinois State Gallery and Illinois Artisans Gift Shop on the second level. You can get a sandwich or a cup of coffee on the lower level.

**Monument with Standing Beast,** gracing the plaza, has significant ties to Chicago art. This exhibition by the French artist Jean Dubuffet was mounted in Chicago in 1984. Dubuffet worked in a style called L'ART BRUT, or "art in the raw." He rejected traditional concepts of personal beauty and often portrayed people as blocklike, with black lines articulating their shapes, as in this sculpture. The figures also recall the CUBISM of Picasso and Braque.

At the time of an exhibit of his work in Chicago in 1951, Dubuffet gave a series of lectures in the city. He struck a chord with the prevailing artistic sensibility, influencing many Chicago artists and students at the School of the Art Institute who were interested in non-Western, tribal art and were searching for the primitive and the spiritual. Feeling scorned by local art patrons, collectors, and museums, Chicago artists turned to an internalized style of art-making. Dubuffet, the dissenter, became their hero.

Across the street from the James Thompson Center, between Randolph, Washington, Dearborn, and Clark streets, two buildings are connected to become one. The west half is **City Hall** at 121 N. LaSalle St., the east half the **County Building** at 118 N. Clark St.; they are linked by connecting passageways and well-connected politicians. The heavy granite outer walls and the massively large *Corinthian columns* are meant to give the viewer the sense of a seat of power. The lobbies, with *vaulted ceilings* and beautiful *mosaics*, soften the image of raw power—but don't believe the softening, believe the muscle that resides here.

The **Richard J. Daley Center** (formerly the **Civic Center**) is directly across the street from City Hall, between Washington, Randolph, Dearborn, and Clark streets. Chicagoans were incensed when it was first built in 1965 because the color was so red and many considered it ugly. It is

Picasso's sculpture sits in the plaza of the Richard J. Daley Center.

built of Cor-Ten, a type of steel that changes color with time and weather, transforming into the beautiful bronze it is today. Cor-Ten had been around for a long time but had not been used in buildings before the **Daley Center**. The windows are tinted a bronze *tone*, adding to the unity of the overall structure. The architects, C. F. Murphy Associates, understood and executed Miesian philosophy and proportions in creating this elegant building that epitomizes MODERNIST Chicago. The building stands 648 feet, which is quite tall for only 31 stories. Its structural bays are an unprecedented 87 feet wide and 48 feet deep. Offices and courtrooms have unusually high ceilings.

A spacious plaza on Washington St. hosts festivals, markets, demonstrations, dance groups, and concerts, but its truly outstanding feature is the **Picasso Sculpture**, dedicated in 1967. Picasso donated the design for the sculpture to Chicago (the *maquette* can be seen at the **Art Institute**). For many years he refused to explain the subject of the work. Late in his life he revealed that it was a portrait of his wife Jacqueline, who in facial structure resembled the Afghan hounds he loved. The sculpture, like the Daley Center, is made of Cor-Ten steel. As you walk around it, you can see the profile of a long-faced woman and her resemblance to an Afghan hound.

A companion to the *Picasso Sculpture* sits in a small plaza directly across Washington St. In 1981, two years before his death, Joan Miró's **Miss Chicago** sculpture was built. This 40-foot figure is of a woman who seems to be a direct descendant of the wasp-waisted Snake Goddess of ancient Crete. It is built of steel-reinforced concrete, and the hollow areas of the skirt are filled with colored ceramics. The simple form depicting a body looks like an upside-down wineglass. Despite this and the fanciful headdress, the dreary color and heaviness of the figure appear to be the antithesis of the Spanish master's style. Most of Miró's work is magical, almost childlike with its loose, floating, amoeba-type shapes; his work is usually spontaneous, from an unconscious, SURREAL source. Miró had donated the *maquette* to the city many years before, but the project was abandoned until 1981 when the city donated money and formed a committee to raise the remainder of the funds needed to build and install *Miss Chicago*. Miró was unable to travel to Chicago to oversee the production of the sculpture.

Still between Dearborn and Clark streets, but a block to the south between Monroe and Madison streets, you can't miss **Bank One** (originally the **First National Bank Building**). A broadly sweeping curve at the base controls wind and carries the eye up the *piers*, which taper toward the top element that houses the mechanical and electrical needs of the building. From the top and side views of the building, it looks like the frame is set into the structure, and the frame looks as if it could be pried open to reveal what is inside. If the sides could actually be unfastened, you would see elevators, stairs, and ductwork. The bronze windows set against the light-colored granite provide a contrast of *tones* that add to the visual interest of the surfaces.

Bank One's restful, sunken plaza houses Marc Chagall's **Four Seasons**, a five-sided *mosaic* depicting the year's changing seasons. The images are typical of Chagall's dreamlike SURREAL scenes, often expressing the folktales of his youth in Russia. The colors tend to be too pastel and sweet for this powerful building in a neighborhood of powerful architecture. The artist donated the design to Chicago and traveled here for the dedication in 1974. The imagery will give you insight into Chagall's surreal view of the world, but keep in mind that his choice of color in most of his other work is considerably richer and more interesting.

Skidmore, Owings and Merrill created a companion building, **Three First National Plaza** at W. Madison and N. Dearborn streets in 1981. The two bank buildings are connected through an atrium. Although this new building is lower than the first building, the two buildings complement each other in every other way.

▶    Three First National Plaza is green: gardens grow on the roof, which can be seen from the boardrooms and offices atop Bank One (First National Bank Building). Three First National Plaza was deliberately built shorter to make garden and city views available to bank executives and clients from the top floors of the first building.

# TOUR 5

## Early Glory: Carson Pirie Scott, Marshall Field's, the Reliance Building

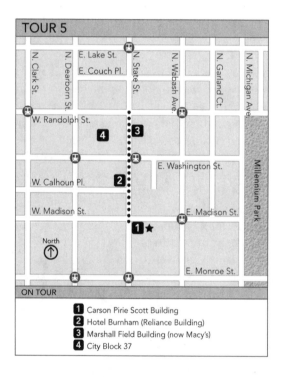

TOUR 5

ON TOUR

1 Carson Pirie Scott Building
2 Hotel Burnham (Reliance Building)
3 Marshall Field Building (now Macy's)
4 City Block 37

The **Carson Pirie Scott and Company** building (originally the Schlesinger and Mayer department store) at 1 S. State St. is the personification of what a department store should be. In recent years the building has been converted from a department store into a multi-use building, but try to imagine it in its glory days as the proud, elegant retail landmark that it will always remain in the eyes of most Chicagoans. In 1899 Louis Sullivan built the first nine-story section on Madison

St., and in 1903 he added the 12-story addition with five bays and the flowing, curved corner uniting the Madison St. and State St. façades. Later additions, moving south along State St., were designed in 1906 by the D. H. Burnham Company and in 1961 by Holabird and Root. Each addition pays attention to and respects the original design. It remains Louis Sullivan's building because of the repeated adherence to his ideals by later architects. The building is made of fireproof steel frame construction in a simple grid of vertical and horizontal *piers*. This grid relates to Mies's **Federal Buildings** (see Tour 2), built 60 years later. The base has two stories comprised of large show-and-tell display windows.

The recessed *Chicago windows* of the upper floors rhythmically repeat their transparent shapes in reflective bands across the surface. A *cornice* tops the structure; the original

The classic Carson Pirie Scott building by Louis Sullivan.

cornice was removed in the 1940s, but because of a brilliant restoration effort in 2005–2006 the cornice was restored to its original depth along with the top, recessed windows, and grand *Corinthian columns*. Be sure also to look at Carson's from across the street to view this architectural legacy in its entirety.

▶   Take a few moments to look at the intertwining cast-iron forms of nature that adorn the rounded front entry where State and Madison streets intersect. The designs, strongly influenced by *medieval illuminated manuscripts*, also appear above the first- and second-story windows. These free-flowing iron representations of natural forms express the idea Louis Sullivan often spoke of, how architecture is a poetic depiction of nature. This building is a pure blend of nature, art, and architecture. Step inside the darkly paneled entryway from the rotunda doors and you feel cocooned in the relatively small, rounded vestibule. Hopefully Carson's will be open when you visit and you can continue your journey through the inner doors, because the doors open up to the brightly lit first floor, which spreads out before you in seemingly endless light.

Move north down State St., remaining on the east side of the street and stopping on the southeast corner at Washington St. before you reach the **Marshall Field and Company** building (now **Macy's**). Look across State St. at the **Hotel Burnham** (formerly the **Reliance Building**), originally identified as 32 N. State St. but now called 1 W. Washington St. Looking at it from across the street gives you a sense of its overall delicacy and elegance. This grande dame of glassy architecture was once faded, shabby, and dirt-encrusted though still gorgeous. The owners could not afford the millions of dollars for a proper restoration, but the City of Chicago, under Mayor Richard M. Daley, bought the building in 1993. The restoration by the McClier Corporation and Antunovich Associates respected and followed the original construction

The Hotel Burnham, formerly the Reliance Building, anticipated the trend toward weightless, glassy skyscrapers.

and décor, bringing back the building's glow and turning it into a charming hotel. The Reliance Building is a *skeletal construction*, with the skeleton bearing the weight of the building on its *piers* and *spandrels*, allowing the walls to become large windows, letting in a flood of light. A light well was built at the southwest corner of the building so that even the basement is bright. The *Chicago windows* alternate between flat and bayed windows, causing the viewer's eye to move rhythmically in and out of space and around the corner. Cream-colored *terra-cotta* with *Gothic tracery* emphasizes the horizontality of this tall, narrow building which was about ten years ahead of the trend toward weightless, glassy skyscrapers.

The development of the Reliance Building is an interesting story. William Hale, a businessman, bought the 1890 building at the State St. site and commissioned a new building to be designed by Burnham and Root. The upper floors of the existing building were rented, and the occupants could not be displaced. John Root designed the basement, first floor, and mezzanine. He raised the upper floors of the building on jackscrews, allowing the demolition and rebuilding of the three lower floors, and leaving the tenants above relatively undisturbed. Carson Pirie Scott then rented the lower floors. When the leases of the upper-floor offices expired, those floors were demolished and the building completed, in 1895. It took only 15 days to complete the steel framing for the upper floors, and new tenants moved in less than a year after construction began. Root died before the second stage of construction began, and Charles Atwood of Burnham and Root took over as chief designer. Hotel Burnham remembers Mr. Atwood by naming its wonderful restaurant at the lobby level for him. Be sure to look at the restored lobby with marble walls, ceilings, and terrazzo floors. The elevators are also a beautifully restored reminder of an earlier era. To pamper yourself after this tour, have a meal at the **Atwood Restaurant**.

The original **Marshall Field and Company** building (now **Macy's**) is across the street at 111 N. State St. It stretches from Washington St. to Randolph St. and from State St. to Wabash Ave. This ROMAN and RENAISSANCE palazzo-type, *load-bearing* structure, a marked contrast to the Reliance Building, was designed to give the viewer a sense of permanence: a rock-solid, safe place to spend your money. It

The famous clock at Marshall Field & Co., now occupied by Macy's.

bears a strong resemblance to many banks built at the same time. The original store was the southeast section built in 1892 by Charles Atwood of the D. H. Burnham Company, the same architect who designed the upper stories of the Reliance Building. D. H. Burnham also built the middle section in 1906, and the S. State St. section in 1907. The north section was completed in 1914 by Graham Burnham and Company. If you have a moment to look inside you will see high ceilings and many decorated *columns*. Arcades in the center are topped by a Tiffany skylight and glorious Tiffany *mosaics*.

Directly across the street from the Marshall Field building is **Block 37**, at 108 N. State St., under construction as this book is being written. The plan for the site, though often changing, calls for Joseph Freed and Associates to build a retail and entertainment segment on the first four floors as well as an underground transit station that will travel to O'Hare and Midway airports. Golub and Company is scheduled to construct a 16-story building housing WBBM-TV, the local CBS station, and other offices. Golub also has plans for two residential towers. The drawings of the building speak of bright, glassy structures.

For many years this site was a vacant lot called **Gallery 37**. It was an ice-skating rink in the winter, and in the summer it had tents where inner-city teenagers learned about and created art. A gallery was set up at 66 E. Randolph St. to sell their work (it can be seen on Tour 6).

# TOUR 6

## Millennium Park and the Chicago Cultural Center

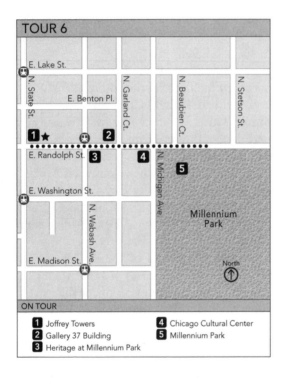

TOUR 6

E. Lake St.

N. State St.

E. Benton Pl.

N. Garland Ct.

N. Beaubien Ct.

N. Stetson St.

**1** ★ **2**

E. Randolph St. **3** **4**

N. Michigan Ave.

**5**

E. Washington St.

N. Wabash Ave.

Millennium Park

E. Madison St.

North ↑

ON TOUR

**1** Joffrey Towers **4** Chicago Cultural Center
**2** Gallery 37 Building **5** Millennium Park
**3** Heritage at Millennium Park

A new building originally called **Modern Momentum** (**MOMO**) but now being referred to as **Joffrey Towers** is at 8 E. Randolph St., at the northeast corner of E. Randolph St. and N. State St. This is the site of the historic but long defunct Masonic Temple. The new building, designed by Booth Hansen Associates, rises 27 floors from the base, which is four floors high with retail shops on the first two floors.

Chicago's Joffrey Ballet owns the third and fourth floors and uses this area as the ballet's permanent home, with offices, rehearsal space, and a *black-box* theater in the building. The roof on top of the first four floors has a garden, and the remainder of the building ascends from that roof.

As you walk east on E. Randolph St. from State St. you can see 66 E. Randolph St. on the north side of the street. This building is where **Gallery 37** is housed. The gallery at the address has some very interesting art pieces done by the Gallery 37 students (see Tour 5). The **Storefront Theater** and a café are also located here.

The **Heritage at Millennium Park,** 130 N. Garland Ct., a 59-story condominium building on the south side of Randolph St., looms over the **Chicago Cultural Center** and overlooks **Millennium Park**. Solomon, Cordwell, Buenz and Associates designed the south end of the Heritage to be 27 stories high, these dimensions relating well to the other buildings on Michigan Ave. Later, when you reach Millennium Park you can see how the slender *piers* carry your eye upward from the *Corinthian columns* of the Chicago Cultural Center. The north end soars 59 stories. From Millennium Park you can see how the Heritage faces the park and the lake, relating to the dramatic curves of Frank Gehry's **Jay Pritzker Pavilion** as well as to the waves of Lake Michigan. The entry to the building, on Garland Ct., an alleylike street between E. Randolph St. and E. Washington St., is humanely proportioned and away from the hustle and bustle of the streets surrounding it. On the Wabash St. side, McGuire, Igleski and Associates have preserved the façades of four historic buildings, three from the 19th century by John Van Osdel and one from 1916 by Otis and Clark. A sculpture by the internationally famous Chicago sculptor Richard Hunt sits on the Randolph St. side. This energetic piece of twisted, curved forms reaching up from a solid base toward the sky, writhes emotionally but manages to remain sophisticated and elegant. The shapes express duality: geometric shapes mor-

The Chicago Cultural Center is filled with treasures inside.

phing into the natural and sensual. The statement **"We Will"** seems to express "we are."

Walk a few steps east and you are at the **Chicago Cultural Center,** 78 E. Washington St. Look at the *Roman arches* with recessed windows. The articulation of the floors recalls the ROMAN Coliseum and RENAISSANCE palazzi: the heavy stone at the first level, the lighter, taller second level, and the *Corinthian-columned* third level capped by an overhanging *cornice*. Notice the protruding and recessing masses that keep your eye moving in and out of space on the Washington St. side.

This NEO-RENAISSANCE structure with many Roman elements was almost torn down in the 1970s. After a powerful protest against this razing, Eleanor "Sis" Daley, wife of the first Mayor Daley, helped save this magnificent building. Built in the late 19th century by architects Shepley, Rutan and Coolidge, it originally served as the **Chicago Public Library**. In the 1960s it was deemed too small to be Chicago's main library, so in 1991 when the larger **Harold Washington Library** was built at Van Buren and Congress streets, the older library became the Chicago Cultural Center.

▶ You must go inside! Enter on the E. Randolph St. side, spend a minute looking at the white marble staircase, the *coffered ceilings* intricately designed and painted in gold, and then travel through the corridors from E. Randolph St. to E. Washington St., glancing at the art shows and paying close attention to the marble walls and *mosaic* floors. When you reach the E. Washington St. lobby, go up the white Carrara marble staircase, noting the *balustrades* inlaid with mosaics of marble, mother of pearl, and glass. At the third floor you will be awed by the Tiffany stained-glass dome and interested in the names of the world's great authors on the walls.

This, the **Preston Bradley Room,** is used for concerts, readings, and meetings, and may also be rented for dinners and wedding receptions. The Cultural Center has excellent art exhibits on the fourth floor as well as those you passed on the first floor. You will have

A Tiffany stained-glass dome in the Cultural Center.

to save the pleasure of the art exhibits for another visit if you wish to see Millennium Park.

► Another interesting note about the Cultural Center is that in 2007 its roof went green. It is filled with Illinois plants and beehives.

When you get to **Millennium Park** (Michigan Ave. between E. Randolph and E. Monroe streets), turn around, take another look at the Heritage building, enjoy the curves, and decide for yourself how the building relates to the Chicago Cultural Center. Then turn back to take in Millennium Park. Millions of people have visited this park since it opened in 2004: visitors diverse in age, ethnicity, color, and geographic origin. In the summer children and sometimes adults splash in Jaume Plensa's **Crown Fountain** while the changing faces on the tall columns spout water. The **Jay Pritzker Pavilion** by Frank Gehry, a *Nike* in flight, is a fantasy of brushed stainless-steel bands that curl and reach, forming a womb for the stage. These seemingly flexible bands connect to an overhead trellis of steel pipes linking 4,000 seats in the main pavilion to

Millennium Park, host to millions of visitors since its opening in 2004.

the lawn that accommodates another 7,000 people. The sound system is state of the art. The best way to see the pavilion is to travel from west to east on E. Washington St. or to approach it from E. Monroe St. through the glorious **Lurie Gardens**. Trying to "see" it as you enter from Randolph St. can be more difficult because so much is happening around it.

The GRECO-ROMAN *Doric peristyle* at E. Randolph St. was reproduced as a replica of the one that stood there in the early 20th century and represents the ROMAN influence on Chicago architecture, though it is out of place with the pavilion and the other POSTMODERN structures. The **Harris The-**

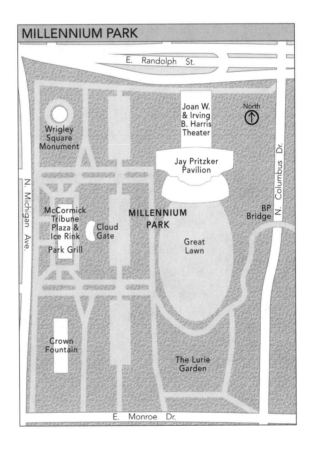

**ater**, east of the pavilion, by Hammond, Beeby, Rupert, Ainge Architects, is a home for dance and Anish Kapoor's reflective, behemoth **Cloud Gate**, popularly known as the **Bean**. Also, do not miss walking on Frank Gehry's **BP Pedestrian Bridge**, spanning S. Columbus Dr.; its sweep, grace, and mere presence are dazzling.

Millennium Park in the winter has an ice-skating rink; in the summer the area is used for an outdoor restaurant, the Park Grill Plaza. The Park Grill itself is an excellent upscale restaurant that serves year round; you'll need a reservation, phone 312-521-PARK. Also in the park is the Park Café, which specializes in providing all the essentials for a picnic lunch.

If you are near Monroe St. after the MODERN Wing of the **Art Institute** is completed, you can enjoy the serene, glassy view of the new building and its companion bridge spanning Monroe St. between the Art Institute and Millennium Park.

# TOUR 7

## South Michigan Avenue

---

If you find yourself at the south end of the Loop, you will want to take this tour. A great work of art by Magdalena Abakanowicz, **Agora**, is in Grant Park at Roosevelt Road (sometimes called 12th St.). It consists of 109 nine-feet-tall, headless figures moving through the space as if in a dream. In ancient Greece Agora was the square where people assembled to discuss politics. Ms. Abakanowicz as a child lived through World War II, witnessing terrifying brutality, and then experienced years of poverty and repression during the Soviet occupation that followed the trauma of the war. The *bronze-cast* figures, each alike but with subtle differences, recall the texture of trees; Magdalena Abakanowicz has compared the gathering of them to a forest. The figures are partly open, exposing a hollow interior, representing the duality of destruction and creativity, of horror, past, present, and future, with hope of filling up the empty spaces. The sculptures were cast in a reddish material that will gradually weather to a brownish hue. They are a gift to Chicagoans from Ms. Abakanowicz and the Polish government.

▶ Spend a little time walking among the figures, gathering your own thoughts about them and how you feel about the *installation*. In this age of quick and easy answers, you may welcome the opportunity to allow yourself time for introspection while moving within this work.

If you have time and the desire to walk, **Roosevelt University** is six blocks north. If you don't have time for walking, take a #3 or #4 bus headed north on Michigan Ave. to the **Auditorium**, part of Roosevelt University, at 430 S. Michigan Ave.

# TOUR 7

**ON TOUR**

1. Agora Sculpture
2. Spertus Institute of Jewish Studies
3. Museum of Contemporary Photography
4. Buckingham Fountain
5. Roosevelt University (Auditorium Building)
6. Fine Arts Building
7. Santa Fe Center
8. Orchestra Hall (Symphony Center)
9. Peoples Gas Building
10. Lake View Building
11. Former Illinois Athletic Club (now belongs to Art Institute)

**ALSO OF INTEREST**

A. Art Institute of Chicago

The sculptures of *Agora*, an affecting work by Magdalena Abakanowicz.

If you are walking, you can also see the **Spertus Institute of Jewish Studies** at 610 S. Michigan Ave. The façade looks like an origami project with folded glass. In deference to the neighboring—and very different—19th- and 20th-century masonry buildings, each of the museum's glass panes was proportioned to relate to the windows of the nearby structures. Built in 2007 by Krueck and Sexton Architects, it is a history museum but also an art gallery featuring Jewish and other multicultural artists. The ninth floor of the museum includes an installation by artist and composer Arnold Dreyblatt, who says his work "uses lenticular technology to create a labyrinthine maze of floating passages drawn from Jewish historical and contemporary sources." Another interesting feature of Spertus is Wolfgang Puck's kosher restaurant.

Columbia College's **Museum of Contemporary Photography**, at 600 S. Michigan Ave., features high-quality international contemporary photographs using a broad range of techniques. The exhibits change on a regular basis. The museum has 7,000 photographs in its permanent collection, which is a who's who of photography, including Ansel Adams, whose scenes from the American West capture the monu-

Buckingham Fountain, built in 1927 to represent Lake Michigan and the four states that touch it.

mentality of nature; Harold Allen, who photographed architecture and its ornamentation; Patty Carroll's brilliantly colored bits and pieces of America; Nathan Lerner, who used experimental processes to impart an ABSTRACT sense to the close-up details he photographed as a member of Chicago's new BAUHAUS; Barbara Crane, who explores patterns; Jerry Uelsmann's SURREAL images achieved by manipulating negatives and prints in the darkroom; William Wegman, who photographs his Weimaraner dogs in bizarre situations; Kenneth Josephson; Cindy Sherman (see p. 192); and Diane Arbus, who captured startlingly candid images of people on the edge of mainstream culture. The Museum of Contemporary Photography shows so many outstanding photographers that it is impossible to name even a small percentage of them.

As you walk or bus to Roosevelt University, glance across Michigan Ave. where, just west of S. Lake Shore Dr. and north of E. Congress Pkwy., you will see Chicago's ROCOCO fantasy, **Buckingham Fountain**, from a distance. Kate Buckingham donated the fountain in 1927 in memory of her brother, Clarence Buckingham. Edward H. Bennett designed this watery showcase to represent Lake Michigan, with the four sea serpents symbolizing the four states that touch the lake: Illinois, Indiana, Michigan, and Wisconsin. The inventive design was influenced by a fountain at Versailles. From approximately April 1 through most of October, the fountain spouts water high into the air from 8 a.m. until 11 p.m. daily, with colored light shows hourly between 8 p.m. and 11 p.m. The POP artist Claes Oldenburg once mused that the fountain was too elegant for the town known as "Hog Butcher for the World" and should be replaced by a giant windshield wiper to clear away the moisture of Chicago's gray days.

**Roosevelt University** was built in 1889 by Dankmar Adler and Louis Sullivan. Originally it was a hotel with an office complex and an auditorium that had—and still has—a state-of-the-art acoustics system. Roosevelt University bought the building in 1947. From Michigan Ave. you can see the influence of Henry Hobson Richardson (of the **Glessner House** and the now defunct **Marshall Field Warehouse**) and the earlier ITALIAN RENAISSANCE palazzi of the 15th century. The heavily *rusticated* stone of the first level relates in complexity of detail and proportion to the people walking by. Notice how the stone of the second level, which has less detail and is lighter in color, and the smooth limestone of the upper levels conspire to enhance the sense of perspective that is an illusion in the human eye. The ROMAN influence shows in the massive stone arches at the base, the lighter arches atop the seventh level, and the small arches atop the ninth level. The building is topped by *columns* and a small projecting *cornice*. The tower at the southwest end of the building was originally the tallest structure in Chicago and housed equipment for the theater. Inside, the post and lintel metal frame is reflected in the lightness of the interior. This fireproof building's décor of plaster, wood, and *mosaics* is extraordinary. The sweeping staircase gives the viewer a sense of the elegance once present in the original hotel. If you can arrange to see the **Auditorium**, you are in for a treat: the grandeur speaks eloquently of a past era. The loggia, the top

Roosevelt University with the Auditorium behind it—a landmark by Dankmar Adler and Louis Sullivan built in 1889.

floor library, and the Auditorium are all worth looking at when you have extra time. If you are interested in touring the building, contact 312-431-2389. Tours are available Mondays at 10 a.m. and noon, at $8 per person.

North of Roosevelt University, the **Fine Arts Building** (originally the **Studebaker Building**) at 410 S. Michigan Ave. was built in 1885 by the architect Solon Spencer Beman. The arches, window placement, and variation of materials show respect for its neighbor to the south. The bottom floors were meant to showcase the Studebaker Company carriages, which were manufactured on the upper floors. When the

Studebaker Company gave up the building as a showroom, it became a center for the arts, with theaters, artists' studios, offices for art education, and music publishers. The old cage-like elevators make it worthwhile to step into the lobby. This elegant old building is showing its age; the School of the Art Institute of Chicago once considered buying it, but the deal fell through. If you need a bite to eat or a cup of coffee, stop at the **Artists' Snack Shop** in this building.

As you move north down Michigan Ave., note the buildings that relate well to the overall feel of the street. The **Santa Fe Center** (**Railway Express Building**) at 224 S. Michigan Ave. was built in 1904 by Daniel Burnham. The variance of some bayed and some flat windows helps create a wavelike façade. The windows are shown off by the gleaming white *terra-cotta* decorations modeled onto the surface. The base is columned with large windows, and the *capital* features porthole windows. The lobby was designed as a light well, creating an airy look with a skylight at the top and a splendid staircase. The Chicago Architecture Foundation keeps its offices here, and its gift shop on the first floor is worth perusing. Shop hours are 9 a.m. to 6:30 p.m., seven days a week. Call 312-922-3432 for information about architectural tours that leave from here.

**Orchestra Hall** (**Symphony Center**) at 220 S. Michigan Ave. has been home to the Chicago Symphony Orchestra for more than eighty years. It is a compilation of styles: NEO-GEORGIAN and BEAUX ARTS, and at the second level it features *Greek pediments* and *Roman arches*. The architect, Daniel Burnham, was a Chicago Symphony Orchestra board member at the time of construction in 1905. Hidden by a lime-stone *balustrade*, the top floor, added in 1908 by Howard Van Doren Shaw, was designed for a private club, the Cliff Dwellers. Harry Weese and Associates remodeled the building in 1967, and Skidmore, Owings and Merrill rehabilitated it in 1981 and 1997. If you are hungry, try the Symphony's elegant restaurant, Rhapsody, or have a drink and a lighter repast at the Rhapsody Bar. Enter them from the **Symphony Center** or at the 65 E. Adams St. entrance.

If you have time remaining on this tour, walk north to see some interesting buildings close to the Symphony Center and across the street from the Art Institute. The **Peoples Gas Building** at 122 S. Michigan Ave. was built by D. H. Burnham and Company in 1910. The **Lake View Building**, 116 S. Michigan Ave., is a slender, white *terra-cotta* building built in 1906 by Jenney, Mundie and Jensen. The former **Illinois Athletic Club** at 112 S. Michigan Ave. now belongs to the Art Institute. Built in 1908 by Barnett, Hayes and Barnett, its façade features a *frieze* showing Zeus presiding over athletic games. A six-story addition by Swann and Weiskopf was added in 1985, but it doesn't complement the original building.

The overall flavor of S. Michigan Ave. is one of grace without gigantic structures.

# TOUR 8

## The South End of North Michigan Avenue

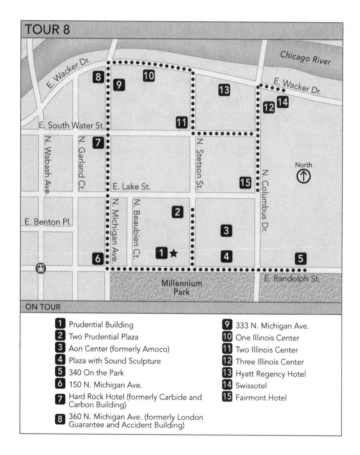

TOUR 8

Chicago River

E. Wacker Dr.

E. Wacker Dr.

E. South Water St.

N. Wabash Ave.

N. Garland Ct.

E. Lake St.

N. Stetson St.

N. Columbus Dr.

North

E. Benton Pl.

N. Michigan Ave.

N. Beaubien Ct.

Millennium Park

E. Randolph St.

**ON TOUR**

1 Prudential Building
2 Two Prudential Plaza
3 Aon Center (formerly Amoco)
4 Plaza with Sound Sculpture
5 340 On the Park
6 150 N. Michigan Ave.
7 Hard Rock Hotel (formerly Carbide and Carbon Building)
8 360 N. Michigan Ave. (formerly London Guarantee and Accident Building)

9 333 N. Michigan Ave.
10 One Illinois Center
11 Two Illinois Center
12 Three Illinois Center
13 Hyatt Regency Hotel
14 Swissotel
15 Fairmont Hotel

When you stand at the corner of E. Randolph St. and N. Michigan Ave., look east toward the jungle of very tall buildings populating the area between N. Michigan Ave. and N. Lake Shore Dr. The first **Prudential Building**, built by Naess and Murphy in 1955, at 130 E. Randolph St., was the tallest

The Prudential Building, left, was the tallest in Chicago when built in 1955. Behind it is Two Prudential Plaza, and to the right is the Aon Center.

building in Chicago at the time of its construction (at 601 feet) and considered by Chicagoans to be a bit of a wonder with its top-floor deck inviting people to view the city from what was then Chicago's highest point. The limestone and aluminum façade fits in with Chicago's architecture of the 1920s. The huge *relief* by Alfonso Iannelli, the **Rock of Gibraltar**, on the south side of the building, is a symbol for the Prudential Insurance Company. This sculptural element humanizes the building, inviting the viewer to study the details of the sculpture from a distance.

The second Prudential building, **Two Prudential Plaza**, at 180 N. Stetson Ave., was built in 1990 by Loebl Schlossman and Hackl. It is certainly not as reserved as its partner. Its spire flying upward, and the chevrons that accompany the spire, echo New York's Chrysler Building. It rises 995 feet. An atrium in a parklike area northwest of the building connects the two Prudential buildings.

The **Aon Center** (formerly the **Amoco Oil Building**) at 200 E. Randolph St. was built by Edward Durrell Stone and Associates and Perkins and Will Architects in 1973. Ostentatiously covered in white marble from a Carrara marble quarry that allegedly provided much of Michelangelo's marble in the 16th century, this thinly sliced marble covering proved problematic and began to fall after exposure to extreme Chicago temperatures. In the 1990s it was replaced by grey granite.

Aon Center's plaza, facing **Millennium Park,** features a sound sculpture consisting of 11 separate units, made of copper rods on a brass plate, that are raised on black granite. Harry Bertoia created it, calling it **Sonambient**. By varying the lengths and thickness of the rods, Bertoia was able to produce a range of sounds: some delicate and gentle, some harsh and sharp. To the east and north of these buildings are a large number of condominium and apartment buildings, a health club, and hotels. Together these structures form a new kind of neighborhood.

A new and interesting building in this area is **340 on the Park** at 340 E. Randolph St., east of the **Blue Cross–Blue Shield Building.** More than 600 feet tall, it has a two-story winter garden at the 25th floor. It respects the rectangular nature of the Loop on its west side and has a slightly rounded wall toward the free-flowing section of Lake Shore Dr. that curves at Randolph. Most important, this is Chicago's first "green" residential skyscraper. It has tinted glass to help control heat and cold, a blooming winter garden, and a huge tank that captures rainwater for reuse in the building's landscaping.

Across Michigan Ave., the **150 N. Michigan Ave. Building** rises at the northwest corner of E. Randolph St. and N. Michigan Ave. It aggressively greets pedestrians but then offers them a covered passageway between Michigan Ave. and Randolph St. It rises upward toward a huge diamond shape sliced from the façade of the building and split through the middle. The diamond ends with a sharp edge on one side and a blunted edge on the other side of the split; they recall knife points, one poised to attack, the other a less lethal backup. If you are at Navy Pier or on Lake Michigan as the sun sets, the diamond shape will seem to capture the light and catch fire.

Walking north on N. Michigan Ave. you will see the **Carbide and Carbon Building** at 230 N. Michigan Ave. It is one of Chicago's best examples of ART DECO architecture, built in 1929 by the Burnham Brothers. This 40-story building is capped with a 50-foot tower that looks like a king's scepter. The *base* is of polished black granite with a black marble and bronze entry. The *shaft* and tower area are a smoky, dark green *terra-cotta*, and the tower (the *capital*) is decorated in gold leaf. The ornamentation is beautifully restrained, bright but never flashy. The darkness of the façade—shiny against smoky—is reminiscent of coal and the gold represents a common reference to coal as black gold. This graceful addition to Michigan Ave. was converted from offices to a boutique hotel, the **Hard Rock Hotel Chicago**. But it still answers to the name of Carbide and Carbon Building.

Farther north, on the same side of the street, is the **360 N. Michigan Ave. Building** (formerly the **London Guarantee and Accident Building**). Its odd shape was dictated by the bend of the river as it crosses N. Michigan Ave. and continues down E. Wacker Dr. The building, designed in 1923 by Alfred S. Alschuler, follows the river, beginning on Michigan Ave., curving into itself and moving back out onto Wacker Dr. *Classic* in style, it has four tall *columns* at the arched entry and huge *Corinthian columns* at the top, finished off with a *balustrade* and more columns supporting a dome.

The odd shape of 360 N. Michigan was
dictated by the bend of the river.

Across Michigan Ave., **333 N. Michigan Ave.,** built in
1928 by Holabird and Root, is a narrow slab with a limestone
shaft rising from a polished marble base. The *piers* run unbroken up the body of the building and tower, giving a sense
of perpendicular slenderness. *Setbacks* near the top break the
unrelieved verticality. The building was influenced by the
Eliel Saarinen design that placed second in the 1922 **Tribune
Tower** competition.

East of 333 N. Michigan Ave. is a hodgepodge of
constructions, a mixed-use city-within-a-city. Three state
buildings—**One Illinois Center** at 111 E. Wacker Dr., **Two
Illinois Center** at 233 N. Michigan Ave., and **Three Illinois
Center** at 303 E. Wacker Dr.—share space with a cumber-
some-looking hotel, office buildings, and a fire station. One
and Two, graceful glass-and-steel structures, were designed

by the office of Mies van der Rohe in 1970 and 1973. Illinois Three was designed in 1980 by Fujikawa Johnson and Associates, who respected the two other Miesian buildings in their work on this building and the nearby fire station. Glance east and, in addition to the **Hyatt Regency Hotel** next to the Illinois buildings, you can see the **Swissotel** and the **Fairmont Hotel**. While it may be difficult to appreciate the beauty of these buildings in this crowded and confusing area, this development has always been economically successful.

▶    As people moved out of the city and toward the suburbs, the doomsayers predicted the end of the Loop, Michigan Ave., and all centrally located commercial areas. Chicago's downtown did indeed experience an initial slump, but city officials authorized a redesign of State St. (more than once) and encouraged new stores, offices, and, perhaps most important, residential condominiums. As you walk this tour, you can see the product of these efforts in the many condominium buildings east on Randolph St., the restored Carbide and Carbon Building (now the Hard Rock Hotel), and the many office buildings and hotels east of Michigan Ave. and south of the **Michigan Ave. Bridge**. In this relatively small area, not as famous as the Loop or N. Michigan Ave., you can see a microcosm of the vital activity that is repeated throughout all the central shopping, business, and living areas of Chicago.

# TOUR 9

## Over the River to the Beginning of the Magnificent Mile

TOUR 9

N. Wabash Ave.
N. Rush St.
N. Michigan Ave.
N. Saint Clair St.
E. Ohio St.
N. McClurg Ct.
E. Grand Ave.
N. State St.
E. Hubbard St.
E. Illinois Ave.
Lake Point Tower **8**
**6**
E. Kinzie St.
**5**
**2**
**4**
E. North Water St.
**7**
N. Columbus Dr.
**3**
**1**
Chicago River
E. Wacker Dr.

E. South Water St.
North ↑

ON TOUR

**1** Michigan Ave. Bridge  **4** Equitable Building  **7** Gleacher Center
**2** Wrigley Building  **5** NBC Tower  **8** Lake Point Tower, to be seen from a distance
**3** Trump Tower  **6** Tribune Tower

Cross the graceful **Michigan Ave. Bridge** to go north onto the Magnificent Mile. The bridge, built in 1920 by Edward H. Bennett, can be raised for boat traffic on the Chicago River. The relief sculptures on the south pylons of the bridge, by Henry Hering, are entitled **Defense**, depicting the Fort Dearborn Massacre of 1812, and **Regeneration**, showing workers rebuilding the city after the Great Fire. The strained

*Regeneration*, a relief sculpture on one of the south pylons of the Michigan Ave. Bridge, depicts the rebuilding of the city after the Great Chicago Fire.

musculature of the male figures in the work must have influenced the workingman torsos in WPA sculptures and paintings done many years later. The north pylons are by James Earle Fraser and honor the **Discoverers**, Jacques Marquette and Louis Jolliet, and **The Pioneers.** The *reliefs* were influenced by public sculpture in Paris that included reliefs on the Arc de Triomphe. During the period when the sculptures were commissioned, it was generally accepted that European art was more informed and important than American art. As a result, the bridge sculptures were acceptable in spite of the work being derivative. The reliefs gave Chicago a highly valued "taste of Paris." Notice how the figures are placed on a "stage," projecting out from the pylons, and how the female "angels" float above the other figures. In recent years the bridgehouse on the southwest corner has also functioned as the McCormick Tribune Bridgehouse and Chicago River Museum, which you can visit May through October for a modest fee. You enter it at the bottom of the stairs that lead to the river from Michigan Ave. and Wacker Dr.

When you look up from the bridge and toward the northwest, a familiar sight and brilliant beacon will be in front of you in this constantly busy, commercial part of the city. The **Wrigley Building**, 410 N. Michigan Ave., is a virginal, pure white NEO-GOTHIC palace housing offices. Built between 1919 and 1924, it is really two buildings side by side with a 398-foot tower that rises atop the taller building. A 14th-floor walkway unites the buildings, and at ground level there is a lovely small plaza between them. One explanation for the building's sparkling white color is that it reminds the passerby of the fresh feeling your mouth experiences upon chewing a stick of Wrigley's gum. The architect, Charles Beersman of Graham, Anderson, Probst and White, left behind a legacy in this, one of Chicago's most recognizable buildings. During the day the sun accentuates the building's white *terra-cotta*, glittering windows, and *piers* reaching for the sky. It is dazzling at night when floodlights illuminate its white form against the dark sky.

On the river, just west of the Wrigley Building, is a tall, slender, newer building with three *setbacks*. The **Trump International Hotel and Tower** provides a glassy, glitzy backdrop for the Wrigley Building and is scheduled to be completed in 2009. The architect, Chicagoan Adrian Smith of Skidmore, Owings and Merrill, designed the building to relate to its closest companions: the Wrigley Building, *setback* one, **Marina City**, setback two, and the **330 N. Wacker Dr.**

The white terra-cotta Wrigley Building, with Tribune Tower in the background.

**Building**, setback three. The **Trump** is formed of silvery stainless steel, glass, and a crisscross *tracery* design, giving the façade depth and texture. Originally designed to be the tallest building in the world, it was altered by the events of September 11, 2001. Nevertheless the building reaches an impressive height of 1,362 feet and is anything but modest. As you look at it from a variety of angles, consider whether every angle is pleasing to the eye.

Across the street from the Wrigley Building, on the east side of Michigan Ave., is the **Equitable Building** at 401 N. Michigan Ave. Built in 1965 by Skidmore, Owings and Merrill, it was influenced by Mies van der Rohe's **860–880 Lake Shore Dr. Buildings** of 1951. *Piers* running up the building articulate the underlying steel structure and divide the windows into groups of four, creating a steady rhythm across the aesthetically pleasing façade. Like the Mies buildings, the proportions and materials become the décor. The top and bottom of the building house mechanical necessities. The building's generous plaza gives pedestrians the chance to catch their breath and have a clear view of the **Tribune Tower** next door.

If you look east between the Equitable Building and the Tribune Tower, you can see the **NBC Tower** at 434 N. Columbus Dr. Built in 1989 by Skidmore, Owings and Merrill, it is an ART DECO building reminiscent of New York's Rockefeller Center.

Behind the Tribune Tower, at the river, the University of Chicago's Graduate School of Business has classrooms, conference halls, and food services at the **Gleacher Center,** 450 N. Cityfront Plaza Dr. Built in 1994 by Lohan and Associates, it has no windows on the west side of the building, where the classrooms are and where students might be distracted by the city views. The other façades have excellent views of the Chicago skyline.

Overlooking Lake Michigan, **Lake Point Tower,** at 505 N. Lake Shore Dr., is a three-lobed, curvilinear building with undulating masses that seem to repeat the motion of the lake. It resembles a beautifully shaped bottle, corked at the top and flexible enough to allow the water to move in three repeated waves. The top floor houses a restaurant, and the west side of the roof offers a pond, a waterfall, a playground, and, amazingly, wooded trails. Elevators are in the center core, and

The idea for a design that influenced Lake Point Tower was first conceived by Mies van der Rohe, but for lack of technology it could not be built until 45 years later.

every apartment has a view of the lake. Window placement was planned so that no resident can see into another's apartment. This reinforced concrete building has bronze-tinted curtain walls and rises from a masonry podium.

The idea for a design that influenced Lake Point Tower was first conceived by Mies van der Rohe in 1919, but it could not be built at the time because Mies's design was so far ahead of the technology necessary to construct it. In 1964 two former students of Mies's, George Schipporeit and John Heinrich, adapted his original design and built Lake Point Tower. The same year, another former Mies student, Bertrand Goldberg, also used the original idea to design Marina City. Luckily, Mies lived to see the start of construction on both projects.

The city plan, written by Daniel Burnham between 1906 and 1909, reinforced the protection of the lakefront, which was to remain forever a park system for the benefit and enjoyment of Chicagoans. Lake Point Tower circumvented the plan by building on riparian rights not owned by the city. The half-acre of land and the air rights were held by the Illinois Central Railroad, which allowed the developers of Lake Point Tower to acquire them.

Moving your thoughts back to Michigan Ave., you will come to the **Tribune Tower** at 435 N. Michigan Ave. The NEO-GOTHIC building has a modern steel frame but is clad in traditional limestone. It rises 36 stories and is topped by *setbacks*, *flying buttresses*, and a lacy tower. An earlier, shorter building that blends with the original picturesque structure was built in 1920 by Jarvis Hunt and was formerly the printing plant.

In 1922 the *Chicago Tribune* held an international contest in search of an architect who could build the most beautiful building in the world to house the newspaper's offices. Set during the time of the BAUHAUS, many entries were MODERNIST, but there were also ART DECO and NEO-GOTHIC submissions. Many architects, historians, and other people interested in architecture debated whether the modern phenomenon, the skyscraper, shouldn't be built in a modernist style. But the Neo-Gothic entry by John Mead Howells and Raymond M. Hood was chosen amid a circus of publicity. Their design was strongly influenced by elements seen in France's GOTHIC Rouen Cathedral.

The exterior walls of Tribune Tower feature "souvenirs" from many of the world's famous structures.

► The exterior walls of the base of the Tribune Tower feature international "souvenirs," small pieces taken from famous structures all over the world and embedded in stone. A few of the places represented are the GREEK Parthenon, the ROMAN Coliseum, the Great Wall of China, the Indian Taj Mahal, and even a stone brought back from the moon. The arched entryway of the Tribune Tower shows characters from *Aesop's Fables*, the tales passed down orally from generation to generation in ancient Mesopotamia.

# TOUR 10

## The Northern Magnificent Mile

Because of time constraints, you cannot look at everything as you move toward the north end of Michigan Ave. at Oak St. This tour will offer information about a variety of buildings but will concentrate on those that are, for good or for bad, most important.

The street has changed considerably since the early 1970s. Before then the Magnificent Mile was a charming, European-type street perfect for strolling. It featured easy-to-look-at BEAUX ARTS, ART DECO, and NEO-CLASSIC buildings, some of which were built around atriums with gardens and others featuring lovely outdoor restaurants encircled by apartment balconies. The scale was humanistic; even the taller buildings gave an illusion of horizontality. A few of those older buildings remain, but many were torn down to make room for huge, multi-use structures. These additions represent both powerful, quite beautiful examples of multi-use buildings along with edifices that bring at best mediocrity and at worst shame to Chicago architecture.

Michigan Ave. has become a developer's dream. While it is still a great street for walking and looking, the pace imposed by the pedestrian crowds can no longer be called strolling. Be prepared to look at both sides of the street as you walk. Remember, most buildings are best seen both from close up and from across the street.

Immediately north of the **Tribune Tower,** still on the east side of Michigan Ave., you pass the **Hotel Intercontinental** (formerly the **Medinah Athletic Club**) at 505 N. Michigan Ave., a ROMANTIC building with NEO-EGYPTIAN *reliefs* and a gold-leafed dome that looks like a large balloon. It was built in 1929 by the architect Walter Ahlschlager and restored in

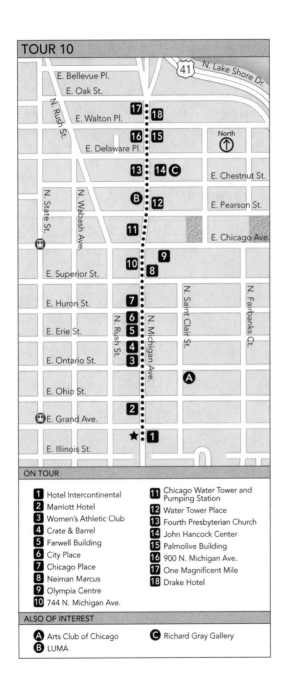

# TOUR 10

E. Bellevue Pl.
E. Oak St.
N. Lake Shore Dr.
41

N. Rush St.

**17** **18**
E. Walton Pl.

**16** **15**
North
↑
E. Delaware Pl.

**13** **14** **C**
E. Chestnut St.

N. State St.

N. Wabash Ave.

**B** **12**
E. Pearson St.

**11**
E. Chicago Ave.

**10** **9**
**8**
E. Superior St.

N. Saint Clair St.

N. Fairbanks Ct.

E. Huron St.
**7**

**6**
**5**
E. Erie St.

N. Rush St.

N. Michigan Ave.

**4**
**3**
E. Ontario St.

E. Ohio St.
**A**

**2**
E. Grand Ave.

★ **1**
E. Illinois St.

## ON TOUR

**1** Hotel Intercontinental
**2** Marriott Hotel
**3** Women's Athletic Club
**4** Crate & Barrel
**5** Farwell Building
**6** City Place
**7** Chicago Place
**8** Neiman Marcus
**9** Olympia Centre
**10** 744 N. Michigan Ave.
**11** Chicago Water Tower and Pumping Station
**12** Water Tower Place
**13** Fourth Presbyterian Church
**14** John Hancock Center
**15** Palmolive Building
**16** 900 N. Michigan Ave.
**17** One Magnificent Mile
**18** Drake Hotel

## ALSO OF INTEREST

**A** Arts Club of Chicago
**B** LUMA
**C** Richard Gray Gallery

1989 by Harry Weese and Associates. On the west side of the
street, at 520 N. Michigan Ave., a developer preserved the
façades of several buildings, including an ART DECO gem, because the city and the Commission on Chicago Landmarks
would not allow them to be obliterated. The result is a shopping mall behind the compromised preservation. Next door is
the **Marriott Hotel** at 540 N. Michigan Ave., a less-than-
mediocre building that replaced another great Art Deco jewel.
Still on the west side of Michigan Ave. you will pass the
**Women's Athletic Club**, an elegant *French-style* building at
626 N. Michigan Ave. by architect Philip Maher.

If time allows, walk one block east from Michigan Ave.
toward St. Clair St. and you will find the **Arts Club of
Chicago** at 201 E. Ontario St. Founded in 1916, this private
club is dedicated to the encouragement of high-quality visual
and performance art. The art gallery on the first floor invites
the public to view the three or four exhibitions available each
year. Throughout the Arts Club's existence, its schedule of
performances, lectures, and art exhibits reads like a 20th- and
21st-century history of the arts: Igor Stravinsky, Philip Glass,
Artur Rubinstein, Orbert Davis, Ramsey Lewis, Daniel
Barenboim, Marilyn Horne, Denyce Graves, Hubbard Street
Dance Company, Carl Sandburg, Gertrude Stein, David
Mamet, Robert Altman, plus visual artists Jean Dubuffet,
Naum Gabo, Constantin Brancusi, and Kerry James Marshall. The gallery is open to the public Monday through Friday from 11 a.m. to 6 p.m. but is closed in August. The club
has been at the 201 E. Ontario St. address since 1997; before
that it was in a space designed by Mies van der Rohe. The
grand, sweeping staircase Mies designed for the earlier space
was moved to the current address.

Back on Michigan Ave., the **Crate & Barrel Store** at 646
N. Michigan Ave. is a building of modest height that holds its
own among the many giants because it has *chutzpah*.
Solomon, Cordwell, Buenz and Associates designed this outstanding MODERNIST building. The bright white and glass exterior is totally honest. A shop with everything inside for sale,

it is transparent, the wares exposed to the street, offering a seductive, visual invitation to come in and buy. The rounded corner moves from the rectangle on Michigan Ave. to the rectangle on Erie St. with grace, uniting both sides of the shop.

The **Farwell Building** at 664 N. Michigan Ave. was designed by Philip Maher in 1927 and is a lovely, small example of ART DECO. For many years it and the building at 666 N. Michigan Ave. were home to the now defunct Terra Museum of American Art. At this writing developers are building yet another huge condominium building with a parking garage on this site. The City Council agreed to the destruction of this historic landmark because the developers will place the façade of the original building on the surface of the new giant. This "stuffing" behind a Hollywood-type front has been used with Nordstrom's, the side of the **Heritage at Millennium Park**, and a wide variety of other buildings in the city.

Both **City Place**, 676 N. Michigan Ave., built in 1990 by Loebl Schlossman and Hackl, and **Chicago Place,** at 700 N. Michigan Ave., built in 1991 by Skidmore, Owings and Merrill and Solomon, Cordwell, Buenz and Associates, are huge and gaudy buildings.

On the east side of the avenue is the **Allerton Hotel** at 701 N. Michigan Ave. It is ITALIAN RENAISSANCE in style with *setbacks* at the top.

Farther north, the POSTMODERN **Neiman Marcus Building,** sheathed in gorgeous red granite, is at 737 N. Michigan Ave. The Chicago influence of Louis Sullivan is seen in a massive ROMAN-style arched entryway that suggests ROMAN overabundance, an orgy of goods inside. Entering the store is a disappointment because it is simply a large room with no extraordinary detail. It is attached to **Olympia Centre**, a condominium building that tapers upward and is also covered in the red granite. The condominium building can be entered from Neiman Marcus or from an entrance on Chicago Ave., redefining the concept of living above the store.

On the west side of Michigan Ave. you will see **744 N. Michigan Ave.**, home to Banana Republic. Built in 1992, it is Robert A. M. Stern's first building in Chicago. Since it is much shorter than most of the new buildings, it has a humanistic feel. It is pleasing to look at with white *columns* and an interesting division of the windows on the façade.

You are now at Chicago Ave. Across the street on the north side of Chicago Ave. are the **Old Chicago Water Tower** and **Pumping Station**, symbols of Chicago. These NEO-GOTHIC castlelike structures were among the few buildings to survive the Great Fire of 1871. William W. Boying-

The Water Tower and Pumping Station were among the few buildings to survive the Great Fire of 1871.

ton designed these rather innocent-looking charmers, finishing them in 1869. Both buildings are dressed in a yellowish limestone. The 154-foot tower was created to hold a 138-foot standpipe, which was removed in 1911. Decorated in the GOTHIC philosophy of "more is more," sometimes they have the aura of dollhouse castles. They stand sentry to remind Chicagoans of what they are capable of and how this beautiful city rose and rebuilt itself. A welcome center is open from 7:30 a.m. to 7 p.m. every day but Thanksgiving, Christmas, and New Year's Day. The **Lookingglass Theatre** has its venue here. A charming but very busy little park becomes part of this oasis from the past. On the west edge of the park is the **Park Hyatt Hotel**.

Between Chicago Ave. and Pearson St. at 820 N. Michigan Ave. is another only-if-you-have-time gallery. **LUMA: Loyola University Museum of Art** has an outstanding permanent collection of MEDIEVAL, RENAISSANCE, and BAROQUE art. It exhibits traditional shows with the artist's work on site, but also mounts other shows of digital images the size of the actual artwork. These images are printed on Mylar with backlighting, providing an interesting alternative method of viewing art.

Moving north along the east side of Michigan Ave. you will encounter a heavy-looking, white, windowless slab that houses department stores, shops carrying everything imaginable, movie theaters, restaurants, the Ritz-Carlton Hotel, and high-priced condominium apartments. This highly popular commercial destination is **Water Tower Place**, named for the historic Old Water Tower. The marble-covered hulk moves as far into pedestrian space as possible, assaulting the viewer's sensibilities with its undistinguished façade. Built in 1976 by Loebl Schlossman and Hackl, it reminds you that it is big and important, and you are small.

Across the avenue and one block north of Water Tower Place is the **Fourth Presbyterian Church** at 866 N. Michigan Ave., a NEO-GOTHIC beauty built in 1914 by the architects Ralph Adams Cram and Howard Van Doren Shaw. The

The courtyard of the Fourth Presbyterian
Church feels entirely detached from the
commercial bustle of North Michigan Avenue.

asymmetrical church has one tower, which is typical of
GOTHIC buildings. The church's peaked arches and *Gothic
tracery* designs lead your eye to the parish house through a
courtyard that feels entirely detached from the commercial
bustle of Michigan Ave. Inside you will find stained glass by
Charles Connick and artwork by Frederic Clay Bartlett. The
church is open to the public Sunday through Friday, 8 a.m. to
9 p.m., and Saturday, 8 a.m. to 6 p.m.

Directly north of Water Tower Place is one of Chicago's
great giants and what a powerful, magnificent building it is.
The first architecture to change the look of Michigan Ave.,
the **John Hancock Center** at 875 N. Michigan Ave. was
built in 1969 by the architects Skidmore, Owings and Merrill
and the engineer Fazlur R. Khan. It seems to personify

The engineering and architecture of the John Hancock Center seem to personify Chicago: tough, brawny, and brainy.

Chicago: tough, brawny, and brainy. The outstanding engineering and architectural creativity make it monumental, beautiful, and solid. It is 100 stories high and tapers upward toward the television and radio antennae atop it, bringing its height to almost 1,500 feet. The braces that crisscross the building add stability and, surprisingly, a touch of humanity by framing individual groups of windows. "Big John" grows from a sunken plaza that is slightly too small for the great proportions of the building. It is a multi-use building with shops, offices, and condominiums. The only elements that mar this simple, important building are a fancy copper "awning" extending into the plaza from the entryway of a restaurant, and a dreadful-looking, difficult-to-maneuver parking garage behind it.

Inside the Hancock is one of Chicago's finest art galleries, the **Richard Gray Gallery**, located in Suite 234. It is worth visiting if time permits or you can make a special trip. The gallery began in Chicago in 1963 and is now located in both Chicago and New York. It always has a one-artist or group show mounted in the space, and represents such artists as Degas, Caillebotte, Picasso, Matisse, Duchamp, Albers, Dubuffet, Pollock, Kline, Lichtenstein, Oldenburg, Johns, Cornell, Moore, and many others. Gray also shows younger artists, many who are known and some not yet celebrated.

The **Palmolive Building** (formerly the **Playboy Building** from 1965 to 1989, and before that the Palmolive Building), on the east side of the street at 919 N. Michigan Ave., was built in 1929 in the ART DECO style. Designed by Holabird and Root, it has powerful *setbacks* giving it a great sense of movement in and out of space. One of the interesting things about this building is the 150-foot beacon on top of the building that used to welcome and guide airplanes into Chicago. It was turned off in 1981 when newer, taller buildings surrounding it blocked the beam of light. This building in particular should be viewed from across the street in order to see the setbacks.

On the west side of Michigan Ave. is **900 N. Michigan Ave.**, or the **Bloomingdale's Building**. A marvel of engineering, it is less successful aesthetically. This hulk of a building moves ponderously from Michigan Ave. to Rush St. down Walton St. and Delaware Pl. It houses Bloomingdale's department store, many other high-end shops, a very large parking garage, restaurants, offices, the Four Seasons Hotel, and condominium apartments. Huge and asymmetrical, with elevator shafts scattered throughout, it posed structural problems in its design, many of which were solved by using steel framing for the base, giving the lower retail and office floors large, open spaces and flexibility. Starting at the 30th floor, where spatial flexibility is less crucial, the framing changes to less expensive concrete. The attaching of steel and concrete was achieved by fusing, embedding, and bolting—a complicated job. The engineer was R. Shankar Nair of Alfred Benesch and Company. Despite the earlier buildings of the architect, William Pedersen of Kohn Pedersen Fox—who had worked on **225** and **333 W. Wacker Dr.**—he did not seem to find a pure focus for 900 N. Michigan Ave. A tall, slim tower rises from a low base and ends with four bell towers that appear ROMANESQUE in style and give the illusion that they are a little too large for their perch. Approaching the building from the south, the front and side façades don't mesh—they could be two separate structures from two separate ideologies. Many materials were used but not unified—for example, different types of limestone, marble, and glass, all in different colors. On Michigan Ave. the heavy walls, again reminiscent of the Romanesque style, feature many kinds of POSTMODERN decorations, including a round window resembling a *Gothic rose window*. Could the architect have overreacted to the sterile façade of Water Tower Place? Walk in from Michigan Ave. and notice Bloomingdale's facing east: the Romanesque altar of commerce? Inside, the floors, posing as balconies, spiral up and are supported by simple, stable-looking *columns*. The materials and design inside are far more pleasing than those of the exterior.

North of 900 N. Michigan Ave. and ending at Oak St. is **One Magnificent Mile**. At 940 N. Michigan Ave., it was built in 1983 by Skidmore, Owings and Merrill. It is also a large, aggressive, multi-use building with retail, restaurants, offices, and condominiums. The building would be less intimidating if there were some space surrounding it. Even the *setbacks* don't seem to lighten the building's looming presence.

Across the avenue, on the east side of Michigan Ave., remains the venerable **Drake Hotel**, facing Lake Michigan and the lake-hugging Lake Shore Dr. at 140 E. Walton Pl. (There is no entrance on Michigan Ave.) Built in 1920 in the ITALIAN RENAISSANCE style by architects Marshall and Fox, the Drake resembles a regal throne if you view it looking south from N. Lake Shore Dr. The interior and exterior speak of refined elegance: the lobby, restaurants, and ballroom are gracious and

Entrance to the refined elegance of the Drake Hotel.

subtly decorated. If it is afternoon and you have time, try high tea in the Palm Court lounge.

► You have come a long way. From the southern sentinel of N. Michigan Ave., the Wrigley Building, to the northern sentinel, the Drake Hotel, you have seen a concise history of Chicago architecture and commerce. This experience is different from looking at areas of historic architecture interspersed with newer buildings and ideas. The Magnificent Mile demonstrates a complete restructuring of an area with a few examples of what the neighborhood used to be.

# TOUR 11

## The Chicago River

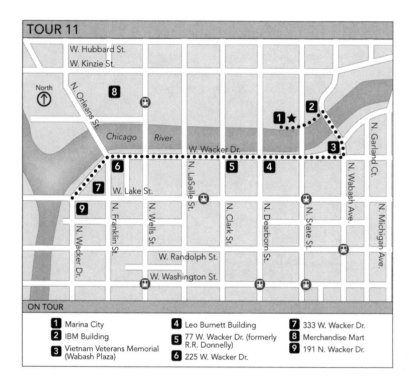

TOUR 11

W. Hubbard St.

W. Kinzie St.

North

**8**

Chicago River

**1** ★   **2**

**3**

W. Wacker Dr.

**6**   **5**   **4**

**7**   W. Lake St.

**9**

N. Orleans St.

N. Wacker Dr.

N. Franklin St.

N. Wells St.

N. LaSalle St.

N. Clark St.

N. Dearborn St.

N. State St.

N. Wabash Ave.

N. Garland Ct.

N. Michigan Ave.

W. Randolph St.

W. Washington St.

ON TOUR

**1** Marina City

**2** IBM Building

**3** Vietnam Veterans Memorial (Wabash Plaza)

**4** Leo Burnett Building

**5** 77 W. Wacker Dr. (formerly R.R. Donnelly)

**6** 225 W. Wacker Dr.

**7** 333 W. Wacker Dr.

**8** Merchandise Mart

**9** 191 N. Wacker Dr.

Begin this walk at the Chicago River at State St., where you will see **Marina City.** It consists of two structures built between 1959 and 1967 by Bertrand Goldberg Associates. The two buildings at 300 N. State St. are affectionately known in Chicago as the "Corncobs." They are built on the site where Chicago was born, the so-called Block No. 1. The innovative towers are each 62-story reinforced concrete buildings with discs resting on *columns* in the core, in a *cantilever* style.

A Chicago icon: Bertrand Goldberg's Marina City, affectionately known as the Corncobs.

The apartments are pie-shaped. The buildings appear to move in, out, and around space, with each apartment having its own cantilevered balcony. In theory, if you live in this complex you don't ever have to leave because it has many kinds of stores, an office complex, a grocery, restaurants, a health club, and a boat dock. Because the design of Chicago is primarily a rectilinear experience, the fully rounded towers of Marina City attracted a great deal of attention in the course of their construction. Plastic forms were used to cast the concrete. The rectangular central cores of the buildings, which contain elevators, stairwells, and utilities, were made by pouring concrete from one-ton baskets hoisted by special cranes. The lower 18 floors are devoted to parking; one floor is nothing but laundry facilities; the upper 40 floors are apartments.

The interesting history of this building began in 1919 when Mies van der Rohe designed three interconnected, round towers. There were no materials available for constructing them, but they remained in the minds of Mies and many of his devotees. In the mid-1960s three of Mies's former students were able to use his vision of architecture in the round: Bertrand Goldberg with Marina City, and George Schipporeit and John Heinrich with Lake Point Tower.

Across the street at 330 N. Wabash Ave. is the **IBM Building** by Mies van der Rohe, completed in 1971. Situated to have the best possible views of the lake, it is built in a dark color of aluminum with bronze windows. Its perfect proportions, humanistic base, and "less is more" philosophy are pure Mies. In the lobby is a bronze bust of Mies executed by Marino Marini, who captured the architect in mid-sentence with a pleased expression on his face.

Cross the bridge over the Chicago River and turn onto Wacker Dr. at Wabash Ave. Wacker Dr. is an unusual street because it moves from the east to the west and then curves at Franklin St., becoming a north-south street.

On the east side of Wacker Dr. between State St. and Wabash Ave., at the river level, is the **Vietnam Veterans Memorial**. A broad, graciously proportioned set of stairs moving down to the river will lead you to a peaceful oasis away from the tumultuous traffic and crush of pedestrians; a handicapped ramp is also available on State St. This grassy park at the river's edge is a tribute to those Chicagoans who died in the Vietnam War. Situated in **Wabash Plaza**, the memorial, designed by Chicago architect Carol Ross Barney with John Fried, has a limestone wall with a niche carved into the stone, where a waterfall cascades lightly into a fountain that spouts water into a pool. The water creates its own music as it flows across a ledge and then moves under the pool to recycle itself. A narrow, black granite rectangle, mounted across the wall and niche, lists Chicago residents who died or went missing in Vietnam. A medallion with an Asian dragon represents the war's service medal and hangs inside the niche. On the ground, beneath the etched names, is a chronological listing of the events of the war, beginning with the first soldier who died in 1959 and ending with the termination of the war. Ross Barney felt the history was important because young people today and future generations must understand the war and its impact. The dust of the city often obscures what is written on the pavement, but you can wipe the dust away with the toe of your shoe. Benches are incorporated into the sloping ground, acting like beautifully proportioned bleachers. Interesting medallions are hung on a low wall next to the pool; the Chicago River laps at the edge of the park. Although not as large or dramatic as Maya Lin's **Vietnam Memorial** in Washington, D.C., Chicago's memorial is beautiful and thoughtful, allowing the viewer time and space for contemplation and respect for the people who died in the violent turmoil of the war.

When you leave the park, walk west on Wacker Dr. and cross the street to 35 W. Wacker Dr., the **Leo Burnett Building**. The famous advertising firm built this 50-story building in 1989. Designed by Kevin Roche, John Dinkeloo and Associates, it rises in three sections with strong vertical *piers* emphasizing its height. Look up at the midsection where the design changes, bringing attention to the floor housing the buildings mechanics.

Continue west, being sure to look at the river which is such an important part of Chicago. When you reach **77 W. Wacker Dr.** (formerly the **R. R. Donnelley Building**), look up at the tall, more or less square skyscraper that has a silver cast to it. It was built in 1992 by the Spanish firm of Ricardo Bofill Taller de Arquitectura and Chicago's DeStefano Partners. If you are passing it at night, enjoy the lighting that bathes it in drama.

Keep moving west down Wacker Dr. and you will be rewarded with a trio of buildings by Kohn Pedersen Fox Associates. The first one is **225 W. Wacker Dr.**, built in 1989. It is slender, well-proportioned, and dressed in gray granite and elegant green glass. It features "portholes," which reflect the portholes of its immediate neighbor to the west. It is topped by four towers and becomes a quiet but perfect companion to the more spectacular **333 W. Wacker Dr.** building next door. Sometimes it seems that 225 is only a handmaiden to 333, but if you look at it carefully you can see its individuality and dignity.

333 W. Wacker Dr., built in 1983, was the brainchild of William Pedersen. Across the river from the landmark **Merchandise Mart**, it reflects the image of the older building in its flowing, curved, green-glass *curtain wall*, respecting the horizontality of the Mart by emphasizing the horizontal lines of its own steel skeleton. The curved Wacker Dr. façade also mirrors the curve and flow of the river at its feet, and the green glass echoes the natural green color of the water (emphasized when the Chicago River is dyed an even deeper green for St. Patrick's Day). The body of the building is so beautifully measured that the proportions become the décor in the Miesian minimal *shaft*. The *base*, consisting of alternating dark green marble and grey granite rectangles, recalls ART DECO forms and defines the lower spaces housing the building's mechanics. Vents that look like portholes are incorporated into the base as a repeated design. Marble and granite *columns* march around the building. The *capital* seems to echo the *setbacks* at the top of the Merchandise Mart. You are drawn by the entrance into an elegantly simple lobby. On the opposite side of 333, facing the Loop, the building becomes rectangular, reflecting the nature of most of the downtown

333 W. Wacker Dr., a beautifully measured building that mirrors the curve and flow of the river.

buildings that are more traditional in shape. Amazingly, every side of 333 W. Wacker Dr. works with every other side of the building while respecting all its neighbors.

The final member of the Kohn Pedersen Fox Wacker Dr. triad is **191 N. Wacker Dr.**, located on the northeast corner of N. Wacker Dr. Note that despite the proximity of 333 and 191, 191 is on the north-south portion of Wacker Dr. Blair Kamin, the *Chicago Tribune's* architecture critic, describes 225 W. Wacker Dr. and 191 N. Wacker Dr. as forming "a pair of bookends that perfectly set off the jewel-like icon at 333." Look at 191, comparing it to 225 and 333.

After comparing these three buildings, move back to the sidewalk in front of 333 W. Wacker Dr. and look across the river at the **Merchandise Mart**. Built in 1931 by Graham, Anderson, Probst and White, it was owned for many years (until 1998) by the Kennedy family. It is imposing, asserting itself as an important part of Chicago as it watches the Loop, the main downtown section of Chicago. It is the world's largest commercial building and was originally the **Marshall Field Warehouse**. Today the primary job of the building's four-million-plus square feet is to showcase the wares of furniture and appliance manufacturers from around the world. It is short and stocky by comparison to its brethren across the river, and like a short lady camouflaging her stature by wearing high heels, it emphasizes its vertical *piers*. It speaks of ART DECO in the *setback* design of the top floors. Your

For many years owned by the Kennedy family, the Merchandise Mart is the world's largest commercial building.

long-distance view from across the river shows the *columns* marking the protected walkway at the ground level and how those columns are repeated in the wall of the river. If you have some free time you may want to visit the first floor of the Mart to see Luxe Home, a wide-ranging manufacturer's display of kitchens and bathrooms. If you do cross the river to the Merchandise Mart, look at 333 Wacker and 225 Wacker from a distance so that you can see the full scope of their beauty.

# TOUR 12

## North and South Wacker Drive

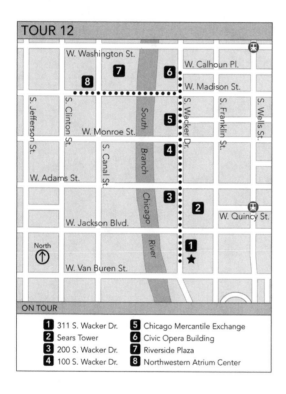

**TOUR 12**

W. Washington St.

W. Calhoun Pl.

W. Madison St.

S. Jefferson St.

S. Clinton St.

S. Wacker Dr.

S. Franklin St.

S. Wells St.

South

W. Monroe St.

S. Canal St.

Branch

W. Adams St.

Chicago

W. Jackson Blvd.

W. Quincy St.

North

River

W. Van Buren St.

**ON TOUR**

| | | | |
|---|---|---|---|
| **1** | 311 S. Wacker Dr. | **5** | Chicago Mercantile Exchange |
| **2** | Sears Tower | **6** | Civic Opera Building |
| **3** | 200 S. Wacker Dr. | **7** | Riverside Plaza |
| **4** | 100 S. Wacker Dr. | **8** | Northwestern Atrium Center |

North-South Wacker Dr. doesn't have the river as its companion. Once the river turns south, it also meanders farther west. Going north and south, Wacker Dr. is a very wide street, a boulevard that gives a sense of freedom of movement as you walk or even stroll.

Begin this tour at the south end of Wacker Dr., at **311 S. Wacker Dr.** Built in 1990 by Kohn Pedersen Fox and Associates, it was at the time the world's tallest concrete-framed building. It has a spacious, charming winter garden. The building is topped by a 70-foot cylinder and four smaller cylinders that recall the turrets atop a MEDIEVAL castle. At night the entire "topping" is lit, and you can imagine Rapunzel from *Grimm's Fairy Tales* inside, letting her very long hair down from the tower.

At 233 S. Wacker Dr. stands an engineering triumph, the world-famous **Sears Tower.** At 110 stories and 1,454 feet, to call it bold is an understatement. For many years it was the tallest building in the world, until the Petronas Towers in Kuala Lumpur, Malaysia, usurped the title. (The Petronas Towers count the height of their antennae atop the towers, but the Sears Tower did not.) The Sears Tower was built in 1974 by the architects Skidmore, Owings and Merrill and the engineer Fazlur R. Khan. The ground floor was renovated and an atrium added in 1985. DeStefano and Partners remodeled the entryways on the east, south, and west sides in 1994. You must look at this wonder from a distance in order to appreciate the full impact of the building.

Before you move away to view the building in its entirety, step inside the Wacker Dr. lobby and look at the Alexander Calder installation, a *stabile* and *mobile* combination entitled **Universe.** Calder's primary artistic interest was always the achievement of movement in his sculpture. He began by creating the illusion of movement in grounded, solid sculptures called stabiles, experimenting his way toward the invention of the freely hanging, moving mobile. In *Universe* he uses both ways of realizing movement, actual and implied, along with different shapes and colors. The forms, colors, and movement are disparate, never developing a thread that unifies. The work often leaves the viewer with the feeling that it is unresolved.

If or when you have the time, the 103rd floor of the Sears Tower is called the Skydeck, and for $12.95 you can view the city from this high point. You enter the Skydeck from the Jackson Blvd. Entrance; it is open from 10 a.m. to 10 p.m. April through September, and 10 a.m. to 8 p.m. October through March.

The Sears Tower has a 103rd-floor skydeck. 311 S. Wacker Dr. is in the foreground.

Now, step as far away as possible and look carefully at this stainless aluminum building with bronze-tinted windows and the *setbacks* that help it achieve a less monolithic look. It is formed with nine framed tubes. All nine tubes reach to 49 stories, then two of them end and the others move up to 65 stories. Only two tubes reach the top. The floors are suspended within the network of tubes, giving the building stability and helping it withstand fierce winds. No wonder the city has a street sign at W. Jackson Blvd. and S. Franklin St. extolling the name of the engineer.

On the west side of Wacker is **200 S. Wacker Dr.**, a Harry Weese building completed in 1981. Weese, who often worked on oddly shaped wedges of land, created two joined triangles, one seven stories higher than the other, presenting a slim silhouette of tinted glass and aluminum painted white. It offers a relief from the unrelenting dark surface of the Sears Tower.

A grid, not unlike a Sol LeWitt sculpture (see pp. 183–184), is **100 S. Wacker Dr.**, also known as **Hartford Plaza**. Built in 1961 by Skidmore, Owings and Merrill, it has a simple, geometric frame of reinforced concrete covered with grey granite. The windows are deeply recessed, which affords them shade from the sun and moves the viewer's eye in and out of space. The constant repetition of the grid on the façade could have been boring, but it becomes animated because of the play of shadows. A second building was added to the south in 1971 by the same architectural firm and is a study in contrasts to the earlier building. It is black, smooth, and with little indication of depth on its surface.

The **Chicago Mercantile Exchange Center** was built by Fujikawa Johnson and Associates in two parts: 30 S. Wacker Dr. in 1983, and 10 S. Wacker Dr. in 1988. These two office buildings have a span between them featuring two huge open trading floors without supporting *columns*, so the space remains unbroken. To sustain all the activity in these two buildings, very thick walls and great columns at the base are essential.

Across the street, the **Civic Opera Building**, located at 20 N. Wacker Dr., was built in 1929. Millionaire Samuel Insull commissioned Graham, Anderson, Probst and White to build an edifice that would house a 3,500-seat theater for opera and a smaller theater for other events, which is now a rehearsal space. The theater spaces are the base for the large

The business tycoon Samuel Insull built the Civic Opera Building in 1929.

office building that rises above them. Some years after the completion of the Civic Opera Building, Insull lost his fortune and died penniless.

The building is ART DECO in style with a touch of RENAISSANCE. An impressive colonnaded walkway runs the entire width of the Wacker Dr. side, providing a protected, enclosed space for pedestrians. The base is a solid mass, creating the feeling that it will effectively support the heaviness of the huge structure. *Columns* run nonstop up the entire midsection of the building and are followed on their upward path by vertical windows. On the river side is a *setback* that creates the image of a gigantic throne. Rumor has it that it was designed to simulate a throne for Insull's mistress, an opera star. This typical 1920s gem is home to Chicago's Lyric Opera.

If you have walked around to Madison St. to see the west side of the Civic Opera Building, you can see across the river

to **Riverside Plaza** at 2 N. Riverside Plaza. It was built in
1929 by Holabird and Root for the now defunct *Chicago Daily
News* newspaper and is another typical building of the 1920s.
It has a great open plaza overlooking the Civic Opera Building. Behind it, at 500 W. Madison St., you can glimpse the giant **Northwestern Atrium Center**, or **Citigroup Center**,
built by Murphy/Jahn in 1987. Unfortunately the beautiful
old **Northwestern Train Station** had to be torn down to
make room for this building. The Northwestern terminal,
still at this site, occupies the lower levels. The huge, spacious,
80-foot-high lobby that leads to the trains is impressive with

The Northwestern Atrium Center replaced the old
Northwestern train station, though the rail terminal still
occupies the lower levels.

a powerful pattern of *columns* and ceiling beams. The building has a glassy blue exterior made distinctive by sensual rounded shapes that cascade down the surface like great, precise waves in a storm.

► Wacker Dr. is built on three levels: Upper Wacker for regular traffic and pedestrians; Lower Wacker for trucks delivering goods to offices, hotels, and restaurants; and really low Wacker, near the eastern end of Wacker Dr., for service vehicles. This idea was conceived by Daniel Burnham and Edward Bennett in 1909. Lower Wacker Dr. was the scene for high-speed car chases in the *Blues Brothers* film and years later in *Batman Begins*. If you have access to a car, Lower Wacker can be entered from S. Wacker Dr., W. Lake St., W. Adams St., W. Monroe St., and others around the Loop. It's a very interesting part of the city, but watch where you are going because the road's twists and turns can be confusing.

# TOUR 13

## Hyde Park and the University of Chicago

Take the #6 bus or the #28 Express bus from
Michigan Ave. to S. Stony Island Ave. and 59th
St. (the Midway Plaisance). Walk five blocks
west to S. Woodlawn Ave.

Tours 13 and 14 are each one-hour long once
you reach Hyde Park. If you have a car, you can
probably see the outsides of the buildings in both
of these tours (Hyde Park and Kenwood) in just
one hour. If you take public transportation, you
will be able to walk only one of the tours.

Hyde Park was the first suburb of Chicago, a one-mile-
square mecca for the affluent. Just seven miles south of the
Loop and situated on the lake, it was a perfect location for the
large, lavish homes of the wealthy. It became part of Chicago
in 1889 and was joined by its most famous neighbor, the University of Chicago, which was financed by John D. Rockefeller, in the 1890s.

Today the Hyde Park neighborhood reaches from Lake
Michigan to Washington Park and from E. 60th St. to E.
Hyde Park Blvd. (E. 51st St.). Many of the elegant old homes
of the 19th and early 20th centuries remain intact in both
Hyde Park and in Kenwood, the neighborhood directly
north of Hyde Park.

If you are coming by car or by bus, you will enter Hyde
Park from S. Lake Shore Dr. at E. 57th St. As you turn off
Lake Shore Dr. you will see the **Museum of Science and
Industry** to your left. This building was originally called
the Palace of Fine Arts, designed by Charles Atwood as part

**TOUR 13**

**ON TOUR**

1. Rockefeller Chapel
2. University of Chicago Business School
3. Robie House
4. Chicago Theological Seminary
5. Oriental Institute
6. University of Chicago Quadrangle
7. Henry Moore's Sculpture "Nuclear Energy"
8. Court Theatre
9. Smart Museum of Art
10. Quadrangle Club
11. University of Chicago President's House

**ALSO OF INTEREST**

A. Lorado Taft's "Fountain of Time"
B. Renaissance Society
C. DuSable Museum
D. Promontory Apartments
E. Museum of Science and Industry
F. Osaka Garden

of the 1893 World's Columbian Exposition. It features pseudo GRECO-ROMAN design and is set on a wide lawn. It is the only building remaining from the Columbian Exposition of 1893.

The architecture was patterned after the GREEK Erectheum in Athens, 421–405. The Erectheum was built on the sacred ground of the Acropolis, which bore religious significance because the highest point of any town was the closest to god. Therefore the earth on that sacred high point could not be changed, and the temple was forced to adapt to the various levels of the land assigned to the architect. It was important to the Greek architect, as it was to all ancient Greeks, that a sense of the ideal was conveyed by all aspects of their lives, including their art and architecture. In order to create the illusion of perfection in the proportions of the structure, the architect visually balanced the sense of weight on each side of the temple, using *columns* to create an impression of the ideal. The Porch of the Maidens used the natural broadness of the female figure (*caryatids*) instead of the less-heavy *Doric columns*, giving the illusion of great weight and compensating for the fact that the building is shorter (on higher ground) than it is on other sides. The lower land on another side of the building has taller, graceful, slender *Ionic columns* rising from its lower base to meet the top of the shorter areas.

The Museum of Science and Industry is not on different levels but uses the variation of several *Doric*-style **Porch of the Maidens** interspersed with other areas featuring *Ionic columns*. This adds interest to the feigned Greek architecture that is capped with pseudo *Roman domes*. If you decide to visit the museum at a later date, you will find a fascinating collection of educational exhibits, many of them inviting the viewer to take part in the display. The museum is open every day except Christmas, 9:30 a.m. to 4 p.m. Monday through Saturday, 11 a.m. to 4 p.m. Sunday. The admission fee is $10, $6.25 for children under 11, and $8.75 for senior citizens. Add $1 to these fees if you are not from Chicago.

Around the corner and a bit farther south, on S. Cornell Ave., is a Japanese garden, **Osaka Garden**, in a lagoon. The garden can be accessed from the south end of the Museum. The **Japanese Garden** was closed during World War II; it was restored, reopened, and a **Japanese Tea House** added in the 1980s.

As you turn onto E. 59th St. and pass under a viaduct, you will see the **Midway Plaisance**, a broad, grassy island separating 59th and 60th streets, both of which are lined with University of Chicago buildings. Begin this tour at E. 59th St. and S. Woodlawn Ave. Get off the bus at E. 59th St. and

Lorado Taft's *Fountain of Time* took 14 years to complete.

S. Stony Island Ave. and walk four blocks west along the Midway to S. Woodlawn Ave. If you were to continue to the far west end of the Midway, just before Washington Park, you would see a massive sculpture in a fountain, the **Fountain of Time** by Chicago sculptor Lorado Taft. The work was commissioned to mark a century of peace between Britain and the United States that began with an 1814 treaty settling border problems between Canada and the United States. The sculpture features more than 100 figures representing young and old, soldier and civilian, and includes a self-portrait of Taft himself bowing his head and wearing a smock. The fountain is based on the lines of a poem by Austin Dobson: "Time goes, you say? Ah no, alas, time stays: we go." The work took 14 years to complete. Because your own time is precious, if you are walking you will have to see the sculpture, formed of concrete (mixed with gravel) and reinforced with steel, at another time. If you are driving you will probably have difficulty finding street parking, but public parking is available at S. University Ave. between E. 59th St. and E. 58th St. You pay at the gate and place the ticket on your dashboard.

Rockefeller Chapel sets the style for the rest of the University of Chicago campus.

**Rockefeller Chapel,** at the northwest corner of E. 59th St. and S. Woodlawn Ave., is a powerful, dominant structure built in 1928 in the NEO-GOTHIC style, the prevailing style on the University of Chicago campus, by Bertram Goodhue. GOTHIC *buttresses* and *pointed arches* adorn the chapel. This limestone *weight-bearing* structure is an impressive way to begin your tour because it sets the style for the rest of the campus. The interior is peaceful and calming as befits the interior of a spiritual edifice. People of all religious denominations are welcomed in this chapel.

Directly across the street from Rockefeller Chapel is the fairly new home of the **University of Chicago Graduate School of Business** at 5807 S. Woodlawn Ave. The architect,

Rafael Vinoly, planned the structure to form an alliance with its closest neighbors, Rockefeller Chapel and Frank Lloyd Wright's **Robie House**, which is directly north of it. The *cantilevered* design accentuated with wide bands of limestone reflects Wright's pursuit of the horizontal PRAIRIE STYLE. The use of limestone and many windows adhere to the GOTHIC style of Rockefeller Chapel as well as to most of the original buildings on the campus. The 415,000-square-foot building gives the business school plenty of space for classrooms, offices, a food-service area, a student meeting area with a GOTHIC–like limestone fireplace and wood paneling, a six-story atrium, and a winter garden with wonderfully bundled but delicate *columns* ending in *ribbed-groined Gothic arches*. A clever salute to the contemporary world is accomplished by filling the spaces between the ribbed arches with glass.

Across the street, directly north of the Business School, is Frank Lloyd Wright's PRAIRIE-STYLE **Robie House** at 5757 S. Woodlawn Ave. Although built on a very narrow piece of land, it conveys a feeling of expansiveness. Tours are at 11 a.m. and 1 and 3 p.m. daily. Or, when you have time, you can arrange a tour of the house for 10 or more people by calling 773-834-1361. For this one-hour tour we will look just at the exterior.

Wright designed this home in 1906 for the Robie family, owners of the bicycle manufacturing firm that later became Schwinn. One of Wright's philosophies in Prairie-Style architecture was to follow the lines of the existing land, assuring that house and nature became one. The rectangular masses of the Robie House have a central core, a chimney, leading inside to a large fireplace from which the living and dining rooms emanate outward. The horizontality of the building is enhanced by narrow bricks with horizontal stripes of limestone defining the levels. Originally the grout between the bricks was light when applied to the horizontal pattern. When the grout was used vertically it was red, similar to the color of the brick, blurring the vertical lines while emphasizing the hori-

Frank Lloyd Wright's famous Robie House, designed in 1906.

zontal lines. When the Robie House was restored, using red grout was found to be prohibitively expensive, so most of the grouting was done in the lighter color. The windows were placed high and surrounded by overhanging balconies, made of reinforced concrete with steel girders, to give the occupants maximum light as well as maximum privacy. Those inside the house can see out, but no one can look in without climbing to the balcony. The front balcony is shaped like the prow of a ship and was used for entertaining. A device in the floor mechanically brought food and drinks to the party. The children's playroom and the billiards room were at the bottom level and protected from view by a wall similar in shape to the balconies. Balconies seem to be the theme of the house. Remember that the large building behind the Robie House, the **Chicago Theological Seminary**, built in 1926 by Riddle and Riddle Architects, was not there when the Robies built. Try to visualize how the home looked with empty land around it.

The home's entry is hidden away from the front of the house (a favorite device of Wright's to keep away casual observers). You may be able to enter, and if you do, you will find a low, rather dark entry hall. Once inside, ask if you may go up the narrow stairway to see one of Wright's ingenious features: how the dim light of the entry opens up into the bright, expansive space of the living and dining rooms. Wright also designed the furniture and dishes, and the clothes Mrs. Robie wore for entertaining. When the Robies lost their money, they had to sell the house and their business several years after the house was built. It was speculated that one of the causes of their financial trouble was the high cost of building their dream house. The Robie House is now owned by the University of Chicago and houses university offices.

When you leave the Robie House, turn west down E. 58th St. to the **Oriental Institute** at 1155 E. 58th St. Built in 1931, it was designed by Mayers, Murray and Phillips in a combination of NEO-GOTHIC and ART DECO styles. The *relief* over the entry depicts civilization's rise from the ancient to the modern world.

The building is typical of the University of Chicago, but the collection inside is extraordinary. This museum is one of Chicago's hidden treasures: many Chicagoans have never visited it, and an amazing number of people have never even heard of it. A minimum of an hour would be required for a taste of the ancient artifacts from Egypt, Mesopotamia, and Persia that make their modern-day home here. A description of the collection may be found in Tour 14.

If you walk directly west and across S. University Ave. you will be in the **Quadrangle**. There are six quadrangles around a central rectangle, meandering between S. University Ave., S. Ellis Ave., the **Midway** (E. 59th St.), and E. 57th St. These park-like areas are encompassed by NEO-GOTHIC buildings and are meant for strolling or sitting and thinking in peaceful surroundings that befit the presence of scholars. The original plan and most of the buildings constructed during the university's first ten years were designed by Henry Ives Cobb. Later buildings by Shepley, Rutan and Coolidge and other architects joined the rarefied atmosphere. The buildings are adorned by *reliefs* and carvings featuring the subjects of history, Christianity, and folktales. The famous landscape architects, the Olmsted Brothers, were one of the firms that created the picturesque grounds, combining architecture and nature.

If your energy and time allow for more, walk through the Quadrangle and go north on S. Ellis Ave. for two blocks to see the Henry Moore sculpture on the east side of S. Ellis Ave. between E. 56th and E. 57th streets. This spot, originally the site of Stagg Field (now rebuilt in Washington Park), was where Enrico Fermi and a team of physicists developed the atomic bomb beneath the bleachers. At this site in 1942 they created the first self-sustaining controlled nuclear chain reaction.

In 1967 Moore, one of England's most famous sculptors, was commissioned to create a memorial for the site. Called **Nuclear Energy**, it is a powerful 12-foot-tall bronze form that can seem to be many things at once: a skull, a protective helmet, and surely a mushroom cloud. It is organic and self-contained, with the forms moving back onto the core of the sculpture. Notice the variety of textures on the surface—some of the marks are ones made by the sculptor's hand. In this work Moore paid tribute to duality: the human intelligence that could conceive of this potential for unlimited energy—that might also bring unlimited destruction. The sculpture is flanked by a good-looking library and a poorly designed building, the **Max Pavlesky Residential Commons**.

One block north you will come to the **Court Theatre** at 5535 S. Ellis Ave., and just east is the **Smart Museum of Art** at 5550 S. Greenwood Ave. The Court Theatre was built in 1981 by Harry Weese and Associates and the Smart Museum in 1974 by Edward Larrabee Barnes. Simple buildings on the outside, they house exceptional talent within their limestone walls. The Smart Museum, like the Oriental Institute, demands at least an hour of your time to see the collections, which are described in Tour 16.

Henry Moore's powerful *Nuclear Energy*
memorializes the site of the first self-sustaining
controlled nuclear chain reaction.

If you walk back to E. 59th St. to board a bus or pick up
your car, glance at the **Quadrangle Club**, 1155 E. 57th St.,
built in 1922 by Howard Van Doren Shaw. Notable for the
materials used, its red brick creates a great contrast to the
grey limestone buildings that surround it. It is a private club,
largely but not exclusively for university faculty and administration, where members can have lunch, dinner, play tennis,
or just relax in conversation.

At E. 59th St. and S. University Ave., one block west of
Rockefeller Chapel, is the **University President's House**
built in 1895 by Henry Ives Cobb. Made of pale brick, the
house has a peaked tile roof and dormers.

If you are looking for a place to eat, you can try the Cov-
ler Café in the Business School or, if you have a car, try the

Medici, a well-known restaurant sporting graffiti-covered booths. Historically the Medici has attracted university students. At 1327 E. 57th St., it serves a varied menu, specializing in burgers and pizzas. The Mellow Yellow at 1508 E. 53rd St. also has a varied menu with excellent crepes and quiche.

Sites not included on this tour but worth seeing another time are the **Promontory Apartments** at 5530 S. Shore Dr. This concrete-framed building was Mies van der Rohe's first high-rise, built in 1949. The structure has not weathered well.

The **Renaissance Society** at the Bergman Gallery, 5811 S. Ellis Ave., exhibits CONTEMPORARY ART. The work exhibited at the Renaissance Society is avant-garde, featuring artists who may not have been presented to Chicago audiences.

Try to make a trip to the **DuSable Museum of African-American History** if you have time. Located in Washington Park at 740 E. 56th Pl., you can reach it from the Loop by taking the Red Line El to the 55th St. and Garfield Ave. stop, then transferring to the #55 bus to Payne Dr. The setting for the building makes you forget that you are in the midst of a huge, bustling city. On the lower level, the museum displays the work of African-American artists, such as Elizabeth Catlett's powerful wooden sculpture of a woman's head, Marion Perkins's three white marble heads melding into one another, and Mr. Imagination's **Tribute to Harold Washington**. A magnificent, imaginative bronze horse rears up on two legs with intricate details in the mane, saddle, and at the base. African art and clothing are shown on the first level.

▶ Hyde Park is just one of many Chicago neighborhoods with interesting architecture and art. It is, however, one of the oldest areas in Chicago as well as home to a great, internationally respected university. While this book also includes a tour of the Pilsen neighborhood, we cannot even begin to cover what Chicago has to offer in architecture and art away from the hustle and bustle of the central area. At the end of the book you will find a list of art and architecture that doesn't fit into any of the tours. If Hyde Park, Pilsen, and the list at the end of the book are not enough to satisfy your interest in Chicago neighborhoods, arm yourself with the *American Institute of Architects Guide to Chicago*, choose an interesting neighborhood to visit, call the neighborhood Chamber of Commerce and ask what small museums, galleries, or art centers you might visit in addition to the buildings in the AIA book.

# TOUR 14

## Kenwood

Take the #28 Express bus to E. Hyde Park Blvd. and S. Woodlawn Ave. Walk south for a block to the Heller House. Turn north for the remainder of the tour.

If you are driving this tour, both S. Woodlawn Ave. and S. Kenwood Ave. are two-way streets, but Kenwood dead-ends at E. 49th St. There is a parking garage at E. 55th St. and S. Ellis Ave.

If you love old houses, this tour of the Kenwood neighborhood can be an interesting walk or ride. Take the #28 bus (see above) or park at public parking, available at E. 55th St. and S. Ellis Ave. Begin your walk at E. 51st St. and S. Woodlawn Ave. (the end of Hyde Park, leading into Kenwood). The **Heller House** at 5132 S. Woodlawn Ave. is a Frank Lloyd Wright house on steroids: taller than what you have come to expect from Wright and with more decorative elements. This is an early Wright house, completed in 1897, just before the PRAIRIE-STYLE houses, such as the **Robie House** in Tour 13. Many elements of this house make their way into Wright's evolving Prairie Style: bands of windows; overhanging, horizontal eaves; and a somewhat hidden entry at the side of the house instead of the front. Made of yellow brick, the Heller House is three stories high with simple *columns* at the second level and more elaborate, delicate, short columns at the third level. A plaster *frieze* at the third story is by Richard Bock, who worked with Wright and other PRAIRIE-STYLE architects.

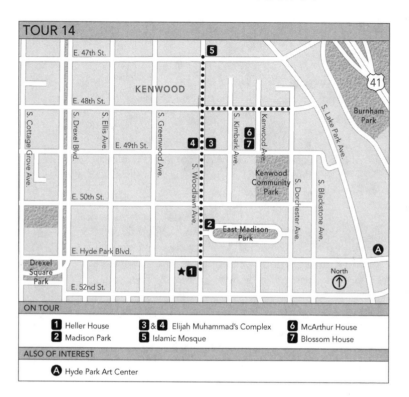

TOUR 14

KENWOOD

Burnham Park

Kenwood Community Park

East Madison Park

Drexel Square Park

North

**ON TOUR**

| 1 | Heller House | 3 & 4 | Elijah Muhammad's Complex | 6 | McArthur House |
| 2 | Madison Park | 5 | Islamic Mosque | 7 | Blossom House |

**ALSO OF INTEREST**

A Hyde Park Art Center

**Madison Park**, at S. Woodlawn Ave. and Dorchester Ave., between 50th and 51st streets, is a wonderful complex of apartments, single-family homes, and duplexes around a central parklike area: a protected, charmingly isolated neighborhood within a neighborhood. Construction began in 1883, continued in the 1920s, and includes traditional apartment buildings, homes, and very MODERNIST townhouses by Y. C. Wong from 1961.

Continuing north, when you cross E. 51st St. you will be in Kenwood. Look at the MODERNIST-style home at **4912 S. Woodlawn Ave**. Built in 1947 by Ralph Rapson and John van der Meulen, this house used old materials rescued from the previous home at this site. Notice the *cantilevered* staircase. The colors were added much later.

An early Wright creation, the Heller House in Kenwood.

At 4855 S. Woodlawn Ave. is the **Elijah Muhammad Home.** On the northeast corner of E. 49th St. and S. Woodlawn Ave., this house and the one across the street on the northwest corner are a combination of MODERNIST and Mediterranean styles. They form a complex that housed the leader of the Nation of Islam, his families, aides, and others. Yellow stone with red tile roofs and stained-glass windows incorporating Muslim symbols make it distinctive. This complex allowed the residents to be a part of a neighborhood and within walking distance of the **Mosque** at E. 47th St. and S. Woodlawn Ave. If you choose to walk down Woodlawn to the Mosque, you will enjoy looking at the gracious old homes, many with elegant ballrooms, that line both sides of the streets. A few contemporary homes have seeped into the neighborhood.

The Mosque is topped by a beautiful dome and four towers for calling the faithful to prayer. Its copper doors are worth a bit of time. After you have looked at the Mosque, walk two blocks east to S. Kenwood Ave. and turn south to 4858 S. Kenwood Ave.

If you choose to save time by not walking to the Mosque, you can walk east on E. 49th St. after seeing the Elijah Muhammad Complex to 4858 S. Kenwood Ave, approximately two blocks away. At 4858 S. Kenwood Ave. is the **Blossom House** and next door at 4852 S. Kenwood Ave. is the **McArthur House**, both designed by Frank Lloyd Wright.

The Blossom House, built in 1892, is of yellow wood with a rounded porch held up by *Ionic columns*. There are PALLA-DIAN style arches above windows and doors, and almost the entire home is Palladian in its strict symmetry. A beautiful, glassed-in, rounded sunporch at the southwest corner of the house takes away from the perfect balance and suggests that

The Blossom House is Palladian in its strict symmetry.

the interior of the home, like life itself, is sometimes asymmetrical.

Next door the McArthur House, also built in 1892, has some horizontal components typical of PRAIRIE STYLE. It is red stucco, rising from a brick base with bayed windows and an open porch.

Both homes have coach houses: Blossom's is on E. 49th St., and McArthur's is behind the main house. These coach houses are where you can truly see the PRAIRIE-STYLE elements that define Wright's later work.

Both these homes and many others around the city and suburbs designed by a young Frank Lloyd Wright are called "outlaw" or "bootleg" houses. Wright was working for Louis Sullivan at the time, and he took commissions for these homes despite the fact that his contract permitted him to work on designs only through the Adler and Sullivan firm. He was desperately in need of more money—he had a wife, children, and a mistress—and took a chance that no one would find out. When the firm discovered his breach, Wright was fired.

The **Hyde Park Art Center** at 5020 S. Cornell Ave. is the oldest alternative exhibition space in Chicago. It was founded in 1939, offering low-cost art classes, galleries for the work of Chicago artists, and great community outreach. Under the leadership of artist Don Baum, the Art Center helped launch the careers of the Chicago Imagists, presenting the first shows of the Hairy Who, the False Images group, and the Non-Plussed Some. The Art Center moved into its own home in 2006, expanding its space, especially the exhibition area and classroom space. Douglas Garofalo reconfigured an old printing plant into the Art Center's new building.

▶   Kenwood was an affluent residential suburb that was annexed to Chicago in 1889. It has some of the largest, most elaborate homes in the city. A current resident is Barack Obama.

Earlier in the century Kenwood was home to both Leopold and Loeb, the notorious murderers of Bobby Franks, who was also a resident of Kenwood. On a decline for many years, Kenwood rebounded strongly in the early 1990s. Like Hyde Park, it features a very diverse population.

# TOUR 15

## The Oriental Institute

Use bus routes from Tour 13 of Hyde Park to
arrive at the Oriental Institute. If you are walking,
go down S. Woodlawn Ave. to E. 58th St., turn
west, and the museum will be at the end of E.
58th St., before the Quadrangle. If you are
driving, turn right off E. 59th St. onto S.
University Ave. Partway down the block you will
find a parking lot, where you pay as you enter
and leave the ticket on your dashboard. If you
cannot or don't wish to walk the stairs, there is a
ramp on University Ave. that will take you into
the side of the museum's lobby. If you don't mind
stairs, walk to E. 58th St. and enter through the
wonderful front doors.

The **Oriental Institute** at 1155 E. 58th St. is referred to as
"Oriental" because at the beginning of the last century,
when University of Chicago archaeologists began their
Middle Eastern digs, the Middle East was referred to as "the
Orient." Step inside and lose yourself in the ancient world.
The museum is free but suggests a donation for entering: $5
for adults and $2 for students and children under 12. Hours
are Tuesday, Thursday, Friday, and Saturday 10 a.m. to 6
p.m., Wednesday 10 a.m. to 8:30 p.m., and Sunday noon to
6 p.m.

Built in 1931, this combination NEO-GOTHIC and ART
DECO building is topped by a *relief* sculpted by Ulric H. Eller-
hausen entitled **East Teaching the West**. *East* is on the left,
*West* on the right, both flanked by symbols of their societies:
a lion, bison, great kings, Persepolis, the Sphinx, and the Giza
Pyramid for the *East*, and rulers, archaeologists, the

Parthenon, Notre Dame, and the Nebraska state capitol (designed by Mayers, Murray and Phillips, the same architects who designed the Oriental Institute) for the *West*. With much to see, the museum will take the full hour. Here we cover only the highlights. The museum provides excellent histories and maps mounted on the walls, with comprehensive explanations of everything exhibited. There are seven main galleries: Pre-History, Mesopotamia, Assyria, Eastern, Egypt, Persia, and Nubia.

The first room as you enter is Pre-History, which will lead you to Mesopotamia, concerned with that piece of land between the Tigris and Euphrates rivers that is now known as Iraq. Evidence suggests that the land was occupied by farmers as early as 8000 or 7000 B.C., and the museum has pieces of early pottery with geometric patterns dating back almost as far. A group of **votive figures** from Tell Asmar, in a case in the middle of the room, are simple, *cylindrical* in style, with broad shoulders and huge eyes. The eyes, repre-

Tell Asmar votive figures from Mesopotamia.

senting the "windows of the soul," originally were inlaid with colored semi-precious stones or shells. The figures symbolized either the gods or ordinary people, with their size indicating their importance. The votives were housed in a *cella* at the top of a *ziggurat*, which was a man-made mountain serving as a temple.

Mesopotamia's first settlers, sometime between 3500 and 3000 B.C., were Sumerians. They built cities and communicated through writing in the *cuneiform* style. They established traditions in religion, architecture, and art that were carried on by other tribes who later ruled the country—Assyrians, Babylonians, Akkadians, and Persians. City-states flourished under kings who were also gods and owned the land as well as the labor of the people. A fierce, militaristic culture reflected the geography of an unprotected land, open to attack.

In the center aisle you will encounter a large, black form covered with *cuneiform* writing and tapering up to a sculpture. This is a plaster cast of the original Babylonian **Stele of Hammurabi** (the original is in the Louvre in Paris). The Babylonians took over a small city-state in Mesopotamia, retaining much of Sumerian culture (1760–1600 B.C.). The founder of Babylonia, Hammurabi, believed in protecting as well as dispensing justice to everyone in his kingdom. He created a code that spelled out the law for all people, high or low born, and the punishment for breaking the law. The laws are written in detail on the *stele*, and the sculpture on top shows Hammurabi handing the code of law to the seated god. The style of the figures atop the stele is Sumerian: *cylindrical*, fleshy, and muscular.

Sometime between 612 and 575 B.C. the king of the Neo-Babylonian culture created a palace complex guarded by the **Gates of Ishtar**. The Gates—dedicated to Ishtar, goddess of love, fertility, and sexuality—consist of thousands of individually made glazed bricks, put together like a puzzle. Two small, original, unrestored sections of the Gates of Ishtar are in this room. The blue of the background is home to calm but fierce lions, and the edges are decorated with rosettes. The Gates feature a quiet, dignified, but powerful procession of bulls, other horned animals, lions, and seemingly fantasy animals. As ancient travelers approached the Gates of Ishtar, they received the message that this enclave was home to powerful people who had the physical power of animals and enough human intelligence and sophistication to create such beautiful, big walls. The animals of the Gates told a great deal about all the people who occupied Mesopotamia: beginning with the Sumerians and carrying over to all the other tribes, the Mesopotamian people had great respect for animals, portraying them as lively creatures with dignity and in artworks often giving them human chores. Most of the Gates of Ishtar have been restored and are at the Museum der Staatlichen in Berlin.

Look straight ahead and you will see a colossal **Guardian** figure from the Assyrian Palace of Khorsabad. The Assyrians were militaristic in their outlook, building huge walls around the palaces and flanking the gates with these immense figures meant to scare off potential invaders. The figures boldly described the people behind the gates who, it was implied, had

A guardian figure from the Assyrian Palace of Khorsabad.

the bodies of animals—powerful, muscular, and threatening; the heads of men, indicating that human strength lies in the brain; and the wings of birds whose strength is their ability to fly away.

Note the three legs of Guardian—no matter from what angle you look at this creature, you will always see at least two legs; no chances were taken that the viewer's position could afford the sight of only one leg, which would make the figure appear weak and unbalanced. The creature's eyes are large and the mouth delicately curved and feminine. The two-dimensional design carved onto the façade becomes one with the three-dimensional forms. Earlier societies and tribal groups were traditionally able to integrate two- and three-dimensional aspects into a unified whole. Later societies have historically had problems with making two-dimensional designs look like an integral part of a three-dimensional work.

The Assyrians (approximately 1000–612 B.C.) considered themselves great engineers (inventors of concrete, builders of enormous palaces) but not great artists, and so they borrowed the Sumerian style for their artwork. They were quite wrong about not being great artists: they used the muscular, *cylindrical* forms of Sumeria but created active, unified compositions with vigorous movement in a manner that was fresh and exciting. The *relief* wall sculptures from Khorsabad flanking the Guardian figure are proof of their artistic abilities. The procession of human and animal figures is animated as they move to pay homage to the king.

In a glass case to your right, before you enter the Assyrian gallery, are bronze bands with reliefs of animals. The work was obviously broken and had to be fitted together with some of the pieces missing. Even though it is only partial, it is an active and provocative work.

In the Assyrian Gallery, to your right, are corridor reliefs carved in stone depicting a lion hunt. The sensitivity of the line and movement is poetic in spite of the violence of the hunt. Note the horses' legs and see how the artist attempted to show natural space with one leg behind the other.

The following Eastern Room includes the Hittites (around 1300 B.C.). Look at the exquisite bronze and ceramic figurines, and fragments of a colossal seated statue, with part of the head on display. A powerful, drumlike form with two-dimensional surface design served as the base of a *column* that must have been impressive in size. Also in the Eastern Room is the Megiddo Collection, with plaques, fragments of ivory, and, amazingly, a small piece from the **Dead Sea Scrolls**.

As you move into the Egyptian Gallery, you will be confronted with a massive sculpture of **King Tut**, king of Egypt 1333–1323 B.C. He became pharaoh at the age of nine, when the Pharaoh Akhenaten died mysteriously. Akhenaten was the first person of power to believe in one god, a radical commitment that caused far-reaching political, religious, and economic unrest. Akhenaten was also an artist at a time when it was widely believed that pharaohs were meant to be, not to do. Tut, who died at age 18, was also a king who "did"—he wrote poetry. His impressive statue is first in the exhibit probably because he is the most famous pharaoh, one of the very few whose tomb was found untouched. He wears a ceremonial headdress, and one foot is slightly in front of the other to indicate movement. Egyptians were inclined to make art on a massive scale to confirm their power and importance as well as to assert their country's power. To them, size did matter.

As you step into this Egyptian room you will see various stages of burial. The first one you encounter is a skeleton in a pit. In the case to your right is a mummy of a young boy wrapped in linen, with a fragment of the painted case remaining at the bottom of his body. Straight ahead are two mummies, one in linen and another in a beautifully painted case. In ancient Egyptian culture the dead were buried with great ceremony that had particular rules.

Egyptian artists were among the greatest craftsmen the world has seen. Perhaps this is because they had to work under such rigid rules (*conventions*) of art that their creativity could be expressed only through the materials available to them and the exquisite way they fashioned those materials. Paintings and sculptures depicting the deceased and the activities they enjoyed in the world of the living were buried with their bodies and may be seen in the fragments of wall paintings in the exhibit. Important possessions they would need in the other world were also buried with the dead (in the earliest days this included servants and special wives).

The Egyptians believed all natural forms had underlying geometric shapes, eventually resulting in a cubic shape because the rectangle seemed to describe the body best. To capture the true look of a person, the artist had to show faces in profile, because the side view best describes the bone structure of the head; the eye from a frontal view, revealing its full shape; the chest also frontal, because that best describes a man's frontal figure (women were not as important). The inside of the legs and insteps of the feet were considered to be most descriptive, and the arms were shown away from the body so they didn't hide any important physical aspect of the person. The pictures were often placed within bands (*zones*) to facilitate the reading of the action, and the stories certainly appear more organized when presented this way. As you look at the wall paintings in the Egyptian exhibit, you can see how these *conventions* were applied. They used *hierarchical* sizes, with the most important figure much larger than the rest, the next in importance somewhat smaller, and inconsequential people, such as servants and slaves, very small.

Egyptian burial chambers for the body, artwork, and treasures, indicating how the deceased wished to live in the next world, started out as *mastabas*. When King Zoser decided that he wanted a burial chamber more distinguished than a mastaba, the architect Imhotep (the first name of an artist or architect ever recorded) stacked up the *mastabas* to create a *step pyramid*. The rough-looking pyramid eventually was refined into the pyramid we recognize today. Inside the tomb was a series of rooms designed to fool burglars into thinking they had discovered the true treasures when in fact the room with the mummy and the real treasures was well hidden and sealed. But clever grave robbers soon discovered, violated, and stole from all the tombs. The Egyptians then built elaborate tombs into the cliffs of the **Valley of the Kings** and the **Valley of the Queens**. The workmen who built them were supposedly kept in the valleys for the rest of their lives so that they would not reveal the locations of the burial sites. But almost all the tombs were found and desecrated; somehow Tut's survived.

Other items to see in the Egyptian room are a bed, a gracefully designed head rest, a stool, and a figure of a god, the **Falcon Oracle**. A hole was drilled into the head of the Falcon, a tube slipped into the hole, and the mouth, being hinged, was manipulated to move while a hidden priest spoke to believers through the tube. Also in the room are examples of Egyptian portraits during the era of the Romans in Egypt. The Romans were interested in showing deep space on a flat surface, so you see a bit of shadow to indicate three-dimensional space in the portraits.

Continue to the Persian Gallery. In 539 B.C. another group of nomads ruled Babylonia, the Persians. They had previously inhabited what is now Iran as migrants. They brought with them small, portable, exquisitely made works called the **Luristan Bronzes**, consisting of bridles, weapons, pole ornaments, and buckles. In the style of the Assyrians, the Persians built huge palaces on raised platforms with *barrel-vaulted* ceilings and a massive type of *column* influenced by the Egyptians. The **Palace of Persepolis** was such a place.

In the Persian Gallery you will see a **Double Bull-Headed Capital** (a head on each side of the *capital* made it certain that the viewer would always have a clear view of the head) and the **Great Bull's Head**, without ears and horns, both from Persepolis. There is also a sensitive *relief* of a lively human head. Think of the artistic sensibilities of the Persian artists as you look at the integration of the two- and three-dimensional designs and the design elements that always bring the viewer's eye back onto the art piece. Alexander the Great wrought destruction on Persepolis around 329 B.C., but a bit of it still exists, and today we can see the scope and planning of the raised platforms with the graceful, large *fluted columns*.

How fortunate we are to have these ancient treasures and understand the intelligence, organizational skills, mathematical abilities, and artistic brilliance of earlier humans. Their creativity and accomplishments are breathtaking, and a reminder that ours is not the first highly intelligent, civilized culture in the world.

Before you leave the Oriental Institute, visit the gift shop— among the most interesting museum shops in Chicago.

# TOUR 16

## The Smart Museum of Art

See bus routes from Tour 13 of Hyde Park.

The **David and Alfred Smart Museum of Art**, at 5550 S. Greenwood Ave. on the University of Chicago campus, is housed in a simple, unassuming limestone block building designed in 1974 by Edward Larrabee Barnes. Perhaps because the blocks have a light, warm, inviting *tone*, the building looks like a museum. The sparse use of windows in the front and back suggests that there are no distractions from the art hanging on the interior walls. The building's modern, geometric shapes set it apart from the GOTHIC campus, but it fits in well and doesn't fight with other university structures. If you are driving, there is a parking lot at E. 55th St. and S. Ellis Ave. Walk across the arts campus—the Court Theatre at 5535 S. Ellis Ave., the **Cochrane-Woods Art Center** (5540 S. Greenwood Ave.), and the Smart Museum of Art—and you enter a charming courtyard with tables and chairs outside the Smart Museum.

Before you enter the courtyard, look at the sculptures outside. To the south is **Why?**, an elegant bronze work by Chicago artist Richard Hunt. The dark, undulating forms reach upward but always, sometimes very subtly, come back onto its core, holding the viewer's attention on the piece. To the north are two engaged, gleaming stainless steel rectangles. As you move around or past Peter Calaboyias's work entitled **Always Excelling**, the two slabs change positions with each other and even change shapes, from one angle an X, from another two diamond shapes leaning on each other. If you're fortunate, the sun will be shining and you'll see one or the other of the rectangles appear to catch fire.

Once inside the courtyard you can see the Cochrane-Woods Art Center to your left (north) and the Smart Museum to your right (south). The Smart lobby features a small self-serve café and an even smaller but interesting gift counter. More important, the back wall has a huge piece by Anselm Kiefer entitled **Lichtfalle** (**Light Trap**). The work includes paint, wood, shellac, emulsion, glass, and a steel trap, all on linen, showing a bleak, charred landscape. The overall work looks like a map of the world, or maybe even of the universe: rough, dangerous, crisscrossed by ribbons that might be roads, and bearing a multitude of signs with numbers. An old steel trap protrudes, containing still more numbered signs. Kiefer, a German artist, was not born until the end of World War II but his work has been obsessed with the death, destruction, and horror of war. He is the heir to the German EXPRESSIONISTS whom Hitler called degenerates, barring their work from public view. Kiefer's work is an ultimate anti-war statement.

A hammered stainless steel sculpture, **Ornamental Rock**, by Zhan Wang, sits to the left of the Kiefer piece in the lobby. Wang placed the metal over a rock and hammered away, creating a heavily textured exterior. Enter the galleries from the side where *Ornamental Rock* is displayed. As you enter, enjoy the ornamental **Elevator Enclosure Screens** by Louis Sullivan outside of the entrance. Sullivan was a master of curvilinear design elements, influenced by *medieval illuminated manuscripts*, especially the Celtic Book of Kells.

The museum has three rooms exhibiting work from its permanent collection. The other rooms are for traveling shows. Although the museum is small, be aware that if you expect to see the museum in one hour, you will not be able to see everything. Also, remember that the museum does sometimes move or change pieces in the permanent collection.

Inside the first gallery is a bronze CUBIST statue by Alexander Archipenko that appears to be a twisting female figure. Despite its geometric forms, it has an unmistakably sensual quality as it undulates, pretending to move. The glass case with several small sculptures includes DADAIST Jean Arp's 1942 highly polished bronze **Siren**, a curvilinear piece of work that turns hard metal into voluptuous forms. Another work in the case is Henry Moore's **Untitled** from 1934, a four-piece composition emphasizing *negative/positive* shapes, making the air surrounding the bronze as important an element as the bronze itself.

A SURREALIST work painted in 1949 by Roberto Matta Echaurren (called "Matta") is entitled **Je M'Arche**. A Chilean by birth, an architect by education, Matta went to study in Europe where he met and was profoundly influenced by surrealists, DADAISTS, Picasso, and ABSTRACT EXPRESSIONISTS. Matta was fascinated by the Earth, and he painted his inner vision of the planet as a living, breathing metamorphosis that was often violent or on fire. His work is surreal and ABSTRACT at the same time, as he paints pictures of his heart, mind, and soul in reaction to nature.

On the same wall is a DADAIST work by Francis Picabia called **Money Is the Reason for Work**, which he painted in 1949. World War I's brutality and its new weapons of mass destruction seemed senseless to many people; if people could be so senseless, their highest aspirations, such as art, also seemed senseless. Dada was an effort to anger people into thinking by espousing an absurd art as representative of an absurd mankind, so Picabia's cynicism made him perfect for the Dada movement—the movement and Picabia were angry at everything, the world was falling apart, and art was dead. Still, note the expert, personal, and loving handling of the red paint in this work and you can sense the poetic side that Picabia tried so hard to hide.

Look for Josef Albers's **Homage to the Square: Green Myth**, painted in 1954. Albers was an early MINIMALIST/COLOR FIELD artist. A member of and teacher at the German BAUHAUS, he came to teach at Yale University when Hitler declared the Bauhaus un-German and decadent, ordering the school to close. Albers's compositions are smoothly painted, with austere rectangles within rectangles. He used the simplest of shapes to experiment with color and *value* and their reaction against other color and/or tonal value. As you concentrate on the painting, the relationship of the colors and *tones* will cause the rectangles to shift space and seem to breathe.

To your left is the dining table and chairs from the **Robie House** dining room, designed by Frank Lloyd Wright. Since Wright was obsessed with the perfection of the homes he designed, how better to achieve that goal than to design everything in his houses himself? The chair backs are tall so that guests at the table are encased in their space without distraction. The light for the table is provided by lamps at the four corners; the dinner party becomes an island unto itself, without outside interference.

To the left of the Wright furniture is a **Fireplace** by Gustave Serrurier-Bovy, completed 1902–1905. It is a wonder of brass, mahogany, and porcelain tiles, and features a mirror and a clock.

Next in this U-shaped building is a small but rewarding collection of Chinese, Japanese, and Korean art. Interesting Chinese **Pottery** dating from 3100 to 2000 B.C. shows how artists used *slip* to paint the designs. A fierce **Guardian Figure** from 650–700 A.D., during the TANG DYNASTY, glares at you, and a table loaded with clay food tempts you.

In the Japanese area are a tiny **Gourd-Shaped Box** from 1900 and a fabulous black lacquer **Tray** inlaid with mother of pearl. The mother-of-pearl design forms fantasy figures circling around a central source of energy.

As you enter the CONTEMPORARY galleries you will see a marvelously colored waterscape, **Harbor in Light**, by American Arthur Dove, done in 1929. The pink sky, gold and grey water, greenish shadows, and sensitivity of the artist's brushstrokes suggest a master painter. Dove's work was influenced by ABSTRACT EXPRESSIONISM but always retained some imagery. It seemed that his quest to understand nature's underlying complexity didn't allow him to erase completely its concrete forms.

Mark Rothko's **Number 2**, from 1967, is a commanding work of art. Rothko was an ABSTRACT EXPRESSIONIST whose work moved toward the MINIMAL but retained EXPRESSIONIST brushstrokes. His emotionally painted shapes of closely associated colors respond to each other and become rhythms of luminous light moving in and out of space. His colors are painted one over another. Each color filters into the one painted over it to give the painting a glow. If you concentrate on the painting, it will begin to move in and out of space.

A part of **The City**, by Walt Kuhn in 1919, borrows the flattened image from Édouard Manet, implied decadence from Henri de Toulouse-Lautrec, and a colorful costume and background from Henri Matisse. The woman's ample body rises from tiny feet, Mother Earth in skimpy clothing.

An **Untitled** canvas is the work of Abstractionist Joan Mitchell from 1961. She painted rhythms of nature and her personal response to the land. A Chicagoan who became an expatriate living in Paris, Mitchell was influenced by the work of Willem de Kooning and Franz Kline but rejected stylistic pressures, instead painting her own vision. She remained an independent Abstractionist all her life. In her day she was a rarity: a woman whose work was highly acceptable.

The Diego Rivera 1930 painting, **Mother and Child**, comments on a mother's concern for her child. The sadness of the mother in the painting expresses Rivera's concern for the future of children in Mexico. The large, simple structure of the figures came from similar configurations of people in many early Italian *frescoes*. Rivera also borrowed from Picasso's earth mothers.

The presence of the artist seems most apparent in drawings. The nature of drawing is to capture the immediate moment, and the line becomes an indication of the artist's mood and character. Three drawings displayed at the Smart Museum are especially prominent: a CUBIST piece, **Untitled**, by Arthur Dove; a watercolor and pencil work by John Marin, **Clouds Overhanging Issy** (1908); and a charcoal **Standing**

**Figure** (1906) by Abraham Walkowitz. A protégé of Alfred Stieglitz (owner of the "291" gallery in New York City), John Marin produced distinctive work. At "291" Stieglitz introduced experimental forms of photography as well as young American painters who were moving into MODERNISM, including both Dove's and Marin's work. In his young days Marin was interested in the wildly energetic aura of New York. He broke apart the skyline and created twisting twirling expanses with diagonal lines rushing back into space. Later he became more interested in interpreting the coastline of Maine, using FAUVE colors and slashing strokes.

A large Magdalena Abakanowicz weaving called **Structure Black** (1971–1972) dominates a wall. The work is powerful and heavily textured. Abakanowicz began her career as a textile artist and this work, done in sisal, becomes a handbook of weaving: it varies from tightly woven, loosely woven, and not woven at all but streaming down like wildly untamed hair. A strongly three-dimensional area toward the center of the work seems to emanate from behind the piece and looks like male genitalia. A slit in the fabric could symbolize female genitalia and offers a peek at the wall behind the weaving. *Structure Black* dominates the room. (See Tour 7 for Abakanowicz's **Agora** sculpture.)

Leon Golub's **Prodigal Son** (1956) refers to the biblical story that confronts selfish extravagance, repentance, jealousy, and unquestioning forgiveness. Golub captures the harshness, tragic consequences, and violence of humankind in his work. His figures are monumental, often majestic as ancient ROMAN statues are, but they feel gouged by time that tries to destroy their dignity. Golub was originally a Chicago artist who worked with a group of artists labeled the MONSTER ROSTERS. The Monster term related to a unique form of heavy EXPRESSIONISM often combined with a highly personal form of SURREALISM. Other important members of the Monster Roster group included Theodore Halkin, Seymour Rosofsky, George Cohen, June Leaf, and Evelyn Statsinger—all educated artists who didn't care about the "proper" way to make art. The influence of Dubuffet, L'ART BRUT is also apparent in Golub's work. (See Tour 4 for Dubuffet's influence on Chicago artists.)

The Martin Ramirez drawing of a horse and rider is **Untitled** (1955): linear, flat, boneless, asexual, and childlike. Ramirez's imagery vacillates between Mexican, Catholic, and North American, with the figure of a bandit repeated over and over again. He also frequently portrayed a Madonna figure. He was obsessed with creating images that he personally wanted the world to see. Ramirez, a Mexican, migrated to California and spent much of his adult life in mental institutions. His work was originally categorized as psychotic art but Chicago art historian Robert Loescher reclassified the work as *naive* or FOLK ART because of its imaginative, intuitive nature along with its symbolism and compositional control.

A 1967 whimsical drawing by Alexander Calder and two 1961 drawings by Alberto Giacometti give insight to the inner workings of each artist. Calder's motivating force was always expressing movement in art. His *stabiles* were solid sculptures designed with great gestures indicating movement, and his work advanced to hanging *mobiles* that actually moved. (See Tour 2 for Calder's **Flamingo** and Tour 12 for his **Universe**.) Alberto Giacometti, on the other hand, primarily a sculptor, was philosophically an *existentialist*. He expressed his isolation in the world through the unsubstantial figures that he sculpted or drew. Often his figures appear to be on the verge of disappearing.

Suellen Rocca is a CHICAGO IMAGIST who showed with the Hairy Who group. **Game**, done at the height of the IMAGISTS' popularity (1966–1967), exhibits Rocca's talents as a wonderful colorist. She portrays obsessive images, often of ordinary items important to her high school years.

Another Chicago Imagist was Christina Ramberg, a part of the False Image group. Her work shows the influence of cheap ads in the pulp magazines of the 1940s. Her figures always seem to confuse the space where flesh ends and clothing begins. **Troubled Sleeve** (1974) expresses the discomfort of putting on a garment the wrong way. In spite of a CLASSICAL, measured, carefully finished manner of painting, the work exudes a sensual, erotic sense of body.

CONCEPTUAL artist Dan Peterman is completely immersed in ecology. His work, in the final room before you return to the lobby, is called **Excerpts from Universal Lab, 1,2,3**. It includes three globes filled with detritus salvaged from University of Chicago research labs. His work is about the idea of overturning the conspicuous consumer culture that abandons tons of waste in our society.

Once again in the lobby, note the sculpture **She** by Kiki Smith, currently on loan. Her themes involve life, death, and resurrection, and she is interested in the symbolic relationship between people and animals, especially wolves.

The Smart Museum is free of charge and open to the public on Tuesday, Wednesday, and Friday 10 a.m. to 4 p.m., Thursday 10 a.m. to 8 p.m., and Saturday and Sunday 11 a.m. to 5 p.m. There are no evening hours from mid-June to mid-September.

▶  Storehouse for the University of Chicago's art collection, the Smart Museum is first and foremost an educational facility. It mounts many interesting and informative shows and has been heavily involved in Asian art, including photography. It is a growing museum, acquiring a substantial amount of new work each year.

# TOUR 17

## The Art Institute of Chicago: 16th Through 18th Centuries

Tours 17 through 21 are of the **Art Institute**'s impressive and expansive collection. In addition to its permanent collection, the museum hosts a variety of shows each year. To see some of the major traveling shows you will need to purchase tickets in advance, though if you are a member of the Art Institute you can walk into those exhibits whenever you wish.

The home of the Art Institute is a work in constant progress. In 1893 the architectural firm of Shepley, Rutan and Coolidge designed a typically GRECO-ROMAN structure that fit the architectural mode of Chicago. Many additions to this building have been made since: the Ryerson and Burnham Libraries were added by Shepley, Rutan and Coolidge in 1901; the McKinlock Court by Coolidge and Hodgson in 1924; the Goodman Theatre by Howard Van Doren Shaw in 1926 (the building is now demolished, but the theater itself has moved to a Loop building); the Ferguson Building by Holabird and Root and Burgee in 1958; the Morton Wing by Shaw, Metz and Associates in 1962; the S. Columbus Dr. addition (with the School of the Art Institute) by Skidmore, Owings and Merrill in 1977; the Daniel F. and Ada L. Rice Building by Hammond, Beeby and Babka; and the Modern Wing by Renzo Piano in 2005–2009. Piano's glassy new addition will be accompanied by a bridge across E. Monroe St. leading to **Millennium Park**.

Enter the museum from the S. Michigan Ave. (at E. Adams St.) entrance, up the broad staircase. On your right is a large and wonderful museum store with a comprehensive selection of books on art and architecture, unusual gifts for adults and children, and jewelry created by a wide range of artists. Plan to spend some time browsing this unique shop. In front of you is a sweeping staircase, worthy of a royal entrance. Proceed to the left to purchase a ticket to enter the museum, where a coat check is also available. Before climbing the stairs or taking the elevator to the galleries, stop at the front desk for a map of the museum. Being a work in progress means that the Art Institute frequently changes its galleries. A work discussed in this book as being in a specific gallery may have been moved. At the time of this writing, major renovations to existing galleries are also in progress, necessitating some rearrangement of works. Also, the ambitious addition of the Modern Wing is under construction, and placement of work in this wing is not yet settled. But you can easily enjoy the treasures in this great museum now if you are armed with a museum map and enlist the aid of the museum guards. The guards are stationed throughout the museum and are friendly, knowledgeable, and ready to send you in the right direction to find the art you are looking for.

Museum hours are Monday, Tuesday, Wednesday, and Friday from 10:30 a.m. to 5 p.m., Thursday 10:30 a.m. (9 a.m. in the summer) to 8 p.m., and Saturday and Sunday 10 a.m. to 5 p.m. From Memorial Day through Labor Day the museum is open from 10:30 a.m. to 9 p.m. on both Thursday and Friday evenings. The entry fee is $12 for adults and $7 for children over 12, seniors, and students. On Thursday and Friday during the summer from 5 to 9 p.m., the museum offers free entry. Children under 12 are always free.

If you are using this book after the completion of the Art Institute's MODERN Wing, you will see the MODERNIST and CONTEMPORARY collections under one roof. If you enter the S. Columbus Dr. entrance or if you are in that part of the building for the restaurants or a lecture, the **Stock Exchange Room** is well worth viewing, with its glowing Tiffany glass and *mosaics*. The Stock Exchange Building in the Loop was designed in 1894 by Louis Sullivan, but in 1972 its graceful beauty was wantonly destroyed to make room for a boring,

second-rate building. A photographer and critic of the demolition, Richard Nickel, was killed by falling debris while
photographing the building during its destruction. The fully
assembled Stock Exchange Room and the Stock Exchange's
front entry arch survive at the Art Institute. The Exchange
Room has been reconstructed just below the Columbus Dr.
lobby. When the MODERN Wing construction is completed,
the arch, featuring *relief* sculptures of Sullivan's interlaced designs, will be installed at the southwest corner of S. Columbus Dr. and E. Monroe St.

Below the Stock Exchange Room is a white-tablecloth
dining room, large cafeteria, and, in the summer, a charming
outdoor restaurant built around a fountain (a sculpture called
the **Triton** that pours its waters into a central pool). The
sculpture, by Carl Milles, is half human, half fish, frolicking
in the pool, capturing strange shells. It was donated by the
Swedish American Committee in 1920. It is a very active
fountain overlooking galleries behind the windows that surround the patio. Lunch becomes an occasion on the patio,
and dinner with live jazz is featured on Thursday and Friday
evenings, Memorial Day through Labor Day.

Now head up the Michigan Ave. lobby staircase and turn
to the gallery behind you. The work will be arranged chrono-
logically beginning with MEDIEVAL art in Gallery 202.

The **Assumption of the Virgin** by El Greco, painted in
1577–1579, will probably be in Gallery 211. This is a MAN-
NERIST work by Doménikos Theotokópoulos, called El Greco
(1541–1614). The *Assumption of the Virgin*, one of El Greco's
finest paintings, was created for a huge altarpiece. It shows the
Virgin Mary rising to heaven in a composition that is divided
into two zones, heaven and earth, both energetically overcrowded with figures. An empty area acts as a bridge between
material and spiritual space. References to spiritual MEDIEVAL
works—arbitrarily proportioned bodies, ambiguous space,
and religious fervor—are abundant in this work.

El Greco was born on Crete, trained artistically in Venice,
and settled in Spain where he became known as El Greco, or

El Greco's *Assumption of the Virgin* was created for a huge altarpiece.

"the Greek." He was one of the greatest masters of MANNER-ISM; his work is beautifully painted, his details super-natural, and his style always consistent with mannerist philosophy. For many years mannerism was out of favor in most of the art world; few individuals or institutions were anxious to have a mannerist work. The Art Institute of Chicago was perceptive enough about the importance of El Greco's work to acquire this impressive painting in 1906 for $40,000. Funds for the work were the gift of Nancy Atwood Sprague. Several other El Grecos may be found in the next gallery: **St. Martin and the Beggar**, **St. Francis**, **Feast in the House of Simon**, and **Christ Taking Leave of His Mother.**

Next to El Greco's *Assumption* on your right is a large, vertical painting, **Crucifixion,** by Francisco de Zurbarán, a 17th-century Spanish painter who worked in the BAROQUE style. As you look at the Christ, his face is at peace but his body is strained and tense. The nails holding his feet to the cross look like bolts, and blood streams from him. The painting is quite BAROQUE in its dramatic lighting and the sensual quality of the paint, so that skin looks like real skin, cloth looks like real cloth. Spanish painters of the 17th century painted dark, simple, flat backgrounds that absorbed the edges of the subject while making sure that the main figure stood out. This device, the *Spanish foil*, also serves to flatten somewhat the three-dimensionality of the figure, a method much admired by Rembrandt and Velázquez, also of the 17th century, and Manet in the 19th century.

In the next gallery is the 17th-century Dutch collection, which includes a Rembrandt. The model for the **Old Man with a Gold Chain** was Rembrandt's father. The elderly man's face shows the struggles and sorrows of his life. The light reveals the psychological perceptions, the watchfulness of the face but remains subtle in harmony with the rest of the painting. The subject appears to be an ordinary man, but he is dressed in sophisticated finery. Rembrandt collected costumes from around the world, using them to impart a universal flavor to his paintings.

Among the many beautiful paintings in this room, none seems to have the inner glow that is so evident in Rembrandt's work. Rembrandt began his career as a typical BAROQUE painter, his canvases featuring great pageantry, super-dramatic lighting, and many excesses. Financially he was highly successful. But he became disillusioned with this type of art and decided the Baroque style was too theatrical and

The model for Rembrandt's *Old Man with a Gold Chain* was the artist's father.

less than honest. He began to observe ordinary people and painted what he felt to be the truth about them and his reactions to their joys and sorrows. He sometimes used natural instead of theatrical lighting. Those paintings of honesty made Rembrandt a master. You rarely see one of his earlier BAROQUE works today. Unfortunately he was never able to sell the honest paintings in his lifetime and was forced to take on students in order to make ends meet.

Another painting in this room, **Young Girl at an Open Half Door,** was originally thought to be a Rembrandt but is now attributed to one of Rembrandt's students.

In Holland in the 17th century there were the Great Dutch Masters: Rembrandt, Jan Vermeer (though there are no Vermeer paintings in the Art Institute collection), and Frans Hals. Their works were masterfully painted and contained deep psychological and philosophical elements. The Little Dutch Masters were also glorious painters, but their message was either sentimental or of the "what-you-see-is-what-you-get" school. Many of the painters in this gallery are by Little Dutch Masters. Pieter Claesz is one of them. His **Still Life** exhibits wonderful skill with paint. The colors and the manner in which they are applied in the still life give a sense of abundance and make you feel that you can reach out and touch the actual object.

Also in the 17th century, Peter Paul Rubens's painting of the **Holy Family with St. Elizabeth and St. John the Baptist** hangs in the next room. Rubens, a true BAROQUE painter, makes great use of brilliant color, sensual textures, theatrical lighting, and the illusion of movement. The textures of skin, hair, and fabric are super-natural and highly sensual. Rubens was influenced by the great Italian master Caravaggio, the first painter to work in the Baroque style.

Although the Baroque style dominated the 17th century, two other painters who had Baroque elements in their work but were not truly Baroque were Nicolas Poussin and Claude Gellée (Le Lorrain). Their work may be found in the same gallery as Rubens or possibly the next room. Poussin's **St. John on Patmos** (1645) presents a contemplative St. John sitting among ROMAN ruins on beautiful land. Everything is ideal, carefully balanced, and emotionally removed from its audience. It clearly states, "Look at me, I'm beautiful, but don't touch." Poussin's paintings were purely CLASSICAL featuring GRECO-ROMAN themes, idealized landscape and figures, and a CLASSICAL ITALIAN RENAISSANCE *perspective*. He was an independent thinker who refused to conform to the Baroque style of the day, choosing instead to portray the measured logic of an ideal world.

In the same gallery is Le Lorrain's **Views of Delphi with a Procession** (1672), one of the first paintings done in the ROMANTIC style. The bent tree and the moody water in the background lend themselves to great sighs.

*Rinaldo Enchanted by Armida,* part of a series by
Tiepolo, one of the most famous of the Rococo painters.

Moving into the 18th in Gallery 215, you'll find one of
the most famous of the ROCOCO painters, Giovanni Battista
Tiepolo. His four-part **Rinaldo and Armida** series is taken
from Torquato Tasso's epic **Jerusalem Delivered**, a story
about the Crusades. The pagan girl Armida seduces the
Christian Rinaldo, thus delaying the taking of Jerusalem.
This is a typical Rococo painting with many curvilinear
movements, color reminiscent of a rainbow ice cream cone,
and a hopelessly ROMANTIC subject matter.

The Italian Tiepolo held a plum job as the Spanish court
painter. His sons, who acted as his assistants, were promised
jobs as court painters after their father retired or died. (Later
in this tour you will see how the artist Francisco de Goya disrupted this sequence.) Tiepolo also did many religious paintings, most of them in museums in his native country, Italy.

Other Rococo pieces, such as Jean-Antoine Watteau's
small **Fête Champêtre** (1718–1721) and François Boucher's
**Are They Thinking About the Grape?** (1747), are also in

this gallery. Watteau used the elements of the Rococo style, including partylike scenes, but probably because he had serious health problems he also showed a more difficult side of life through melancholy or expressions of longing on faces and richer, less pastel color. Watteau's atmosphere is unlike François Boucher's people, who not only party but feel delicious doing so. Boucher's work was a perfect representation of the giddy mood at the court as it tried to ignore what was happening among the peasants.

Also in this gallery is a totally different kind of 18th-century painter, Jean-Baptiste-Siméon Chardin, represented by **White Tablecloth** (1731–1732). Chardin, from a well-to-do family, became enchanted—before the French Revolution—with daily peasant life. His painting is simple, straightforward, and shows a plain repast, placed on a table without elaborate settings, waiting to be enjoyed by an ordinary family. His brushstrokes are evident rather than smoothed, conveying a more casual attitude toward his subject matter. He saw beauty in the simple life.

▶ History in painting: those 18th-century ROCOCO artists who understood Marie Antoinette's "Let them eat cake" together with Chardin, who understood the unhappy rumblings of those less fortunate—the same era but worlds apart, all in one gallery.

The final work on this tour is the six panels by Francisco de Goya, **The Capture of the Bandit El Maragato by Friar Pedro de Zaldivia**. These panels tell how a timid friar is attacked by bandits who had been disrupting the village. The heretofore meek friar throws back his cloak to fight, capturing the head thief. Look at the very modern, short brushstrokes Goya uses in these paintings. The short strokes capture shifting light, influencing many 19th-century artists. As a youth, Goya was asked to leave his hometown because he impregnated a previously innocent young woman. His self-absorbed adventures taught him to advance his career in whatever way he could. He went along with the most popular art style of the time, becoming a Rococo painter. He was designated as the chief designer of the king's tapestry factory, after marrying the sister of the man who was head of the factory. He later became the Spanish court painter, replacing Tiepolo's sons, probably following dishonest politicking on his part. Eventually he saw the shallowness of his own existence. The guilt produced by mistakes of his earlier life propelled him to paint deeper themes that had social impact, such as the work described above. Later still, Goya painted harsher, sharper political commentaries, and eventually he painted the series of the *Black Sabbath* (Museo del Prado in Madrid, Spain), containing horrifying images that gave voice to the nightmares that plagued him late in life.

▶    If you fall in love with a work of art and spend more time with it than you had planned, that's okay. The works described in this tour will still be there when you have another hour to spend. The point of looking at art is to be intrigued, educated, and fascinated. If you have achieved any of those objectives in one or more of the works you see, your trip has been a success.

# TOUR 18

## The Art Institute of Chicago:
## The 19th Century: The Innovators

The **Art Institute** has a magnificent 19th-century collection. It's important as you take this tour to place the paintings in context: the French and American revolutions are over, and the peasants finally have a voice. The aristocratic class may not pay much attention to the voice of the lower classes, but many artists do. The Industrial Revolution takes hold and changes life for everyone. Midcentury a camera, able to create a permanent image of the actual world, is developed, making it less important for the artist to paint or sculpt an object exactly as it looks. For the first time in history there are many, many styles of art representing a multifaceted era.

The Art Institute's collection of IMPRESSIONIST and POST-IMPRESSIONIST works is particularly strong because very wealthy Chicago families traveled to Europe during the summers and bought art on those trips. Unsure of what to purchase, they consulted society-woman-turned-artist Mary Cassatt. Connected by friendship and professional philosophies to the Impressionists and to Post-Impressionist Edgar Degas, Cassatt advised them to buy the new art that was being neglected, often sneered at by Europeans. Chicagoans bought, received great bargains, and eventually watched the once-rejected art become acceptable, thus greatly increasing in value. The Art Institute eventually inherited this work from many local families.

Begin your tour with Delacroix, and move from the Allerton Galleries into Gonzalez Hall. You will finish the 19th century with the late work of Gauguin and the work of Cézanne in Gallery 246.

*Lion Hunt* is a wild and bloody example of Delacroix's restless streak.

An early, important 19th-century ROMANTIC painter, Eugène Delacroix, had a restless streak that led him to seek out unusual adventures. The painting **Lion Hunt** (1860–1861) is a wild and bloody example. The composition of the work, with its twisting, violent movement and sweeping curves, suggests great struggles in sport and life. Delacroix's painting came from actual participation in and keen observation of hunts in Algeria. Look at the quality of his paint applied in short strokes, accentuating changing planes of light. His color is rich, and he sometimes experimented with placing two colors next to each other, anticipating viewers' unconscious mixing of the two hues in their own eyes. (Later in the century this experiment with color theory was used occasionally by the IMPRESSIONISTS and was always employed by Georges Seurat.) Delacroix's work is positioned on the canvas in a manner that invites you into the work and makes you a participant. Many of his most important paintings were of historical subjects. He used ancient events to express problems of 19th-century society.

Large ROMANTIC canvases by J. M. W. Turner—**Valley of Aosta—Snowstorm, Avalanche and Thunderstorm**, and **Fishing Boats with Hucksters Bargaining for**

**Fish**—are exciting. Turner, an uneducated dock worker, felt the emotions of water and the mood of the water within himself. While there are figures, boats, and sometimes trees in his work, the overall feeling of his paintings is one of true ABSTRACTION—about the temperament of the sea.

In Gallery 223 look for two, large, vertical paintings by Édouard Manet, **Beggar with a Duffle Coat (Philosopher)** (1865) and **Beggar with Oysters (Philosopher)** (1865–1867): both paintings tell a great deal about Manet's artistic philosophy. In these two large *Beggar* canvases you

Manet's rejection of perspective is apparent in his *Beggar with a Duffle Coat.*

can see how he flattened his images by using less *chiaroscuro*, using just enough shadow to indicate that the artist was looking at the three-dimensional world. He adopted the dark, flat *Spanish foil* background derived from the 17th-century painters Zurbarán and Velázquez. He rejected *perspective*, not only as a lie but as a waste of an artist's creative time because the problems of perspective had been solved in the 15th century. Manet recognized that the object or person he painted was three-dimensional, but as an artist he was working on a two-dimensional surface; trying to portray the third dimension on a flat surface showed a lack of respect for the reality of the two-dimensional canvas or paper. Manet felt he was being honest, true to the real surface he painted on, not masking the artist's application of paint. He wanted the viewer to see the art as well as the subject matter. Thus he was instrumental in changing the way the world looks at art.

You will find other examples of Manet's work in the next few galleries. Several that might be hanging are **Christ Mocked**, in which a flattened Christ resolved to his fate is threatened and teased; **Self Portrait,** where a steely-eyed Manet stares at the viewer; or **Still Life with Fish,** in which a somewhat two-dimensional but naturally executed fish is waiting to be cooked in a richly painted copper pot that reflects light.

Manet grew weary of being dismissed or ignored, felt insecure about his work, and joined his friends, the IMPRESSIONISTS, who had begun to taste critical and financial success. He was a mediocre but artistically accepted Impressionist. **Woman Reading**, one of his Impressionist works, is well painted, charming and pleasant to look at, but adds nothing to the Impressionist vocabulary. Toward the end of his life, Manet returned to his earlier philosophy and style, creating one of the most beautiful paintings of the 19th century, *A Bar at the Folies-Bergère* (Courtauld Institute of Art, London).

Most artists of the 19th century who saw Manet's work found it valid, adopting his philosophical flatness, at least some of the time. But critics and patrons considered his work undeveloped and Manet himself uneducated because his painting didn't mimic the work of the RENAISSANCE. His influence, however, was such that 20th- and 21st-century artists continue to flatten images on two-dimensional surfaces.

The IMPRESSIONISTS were a group of young 19th-century French painters who were interested in natural light and how it affected form. They could not understand enough about natural light by viewing it from their studios, so they decided to do something revolutionary: they painted outdoors. Pay attention to the short brushstrokes the Impressionists used to break planes of space into light and shadow.

Find Pierre-Auguste Renoir's much-loved **Two Sisters (On the Terrace)** (1881) in Gallery 201 and lose yourself in the lady with the red hat and the little girl in the flowered hat. See the **Two Little Circus Girls** (1879), **Lunch at the Restaurant Fournaise (The Rowers' Lunch)** (1875), and **The Woman at the Piano** (1875–1876). Renoir is like having a light, refreshing, delicious dessert *before* the substance of the main course. He saw only the calm, pretty, easy side of life. His women glow with life and health, his parties look like more fun than other parties, and nature always seems to cooperate. Because he never expressed what the world was really like—the dark with the light, the edgy with the sweet—his paintings are not as important to art history as Monet's, but they are delightful to look at. In his later years, when his hands were crippled by arthritis, Renoir had his brushes strapped to his arms and continued to paint every day.

If it is on display, look at Camille Pissarro's **Crystal Palace.** Pissarro's style tended to be more geometric and carefully measured than that of the other IMPRESSIONISTS. Working with Monet and the others loosened his style, and his nature compositions made his work far less rigid and more modern than it had been earlier.

See if any Alfred Sisley painting is hanging. His work celebrates the ordinary. His are uncomplicated views of what had always been, without imposition of progress or the modern world.

Renoir's much-loved *Two Sisters*—delightful to look at.

Claude Monet is probably the most important of the IM-PRESSIONISTS. He worked in three different ways but always under the same umbrella of Impressionism. His early works will probably be in Gallery 201. An early work, **The Beach at Sainte-Adresse** (1867), shows a slightly overcast day, the clouds changing the color of the water to a faded blue, making it feel chilly. **The River** (1868), of a woman taking refuge from the sun under a tree, is more idyllic, the atmosphere warmer and brighter. In these early Monet paintings the edges were sharply defined, but he moved toward the dissolution of edges as he became more and more interested in painting the atmosphere. Later he began to paint series, **The Railroad Station at Gare St. Lazar, Views of Westminster Bridge**,

Monet's *Haystacks* seem to convey the essence of Impressionism.

**Houses of Parliament**, and **The Haystacks** (the Art Institute of Chicago owns 12 Haystacks, more than any other collection in the world). In his series he painted the same scene at different times of day, under different weather conditions, and in different seasons. These paintings seem to be the essence of IMPRESSIONISM: each unique light, whether because of time of day or temperature, affects the forms of the same subject matter in a distinguishing manner. In each of the series paintings Monet expresses the tensions as well as the beauty that the light brings forward. Later still, when inoperable cataracts rendered him legally blind, Monet moved to his home in Giverny, where he had the water gardens built. He then painted the essence of the gardens for the remainder of his life. The **Water-Lily Pond** series is about underlying structures, light, and atmosphere, and become quite ABSTRACT. They are very beautiful but also speak of a darker, tense side of life as the plants pull themselves from the undergrowth. **Iris by the Lily Pond** and the Water Garden series were painted when Monet could see only large shapes and some color and light. He purportedly said that he regretted his years of sight because he saw too much that wasn't important. His subjects become the quintessential nature of the water, the foliage, and the light. Allow yourself to be enveloped in Monet's atmosphere. If you are interested in seeing more than one work of a series, ask a guard if any are currently being shown in the museum.

Mary Cassatt painted **The Bath** in 1892. It is a typical Cassatt, showing a devoted and adoring mother carefully placing the foot of her tentative child into a small basin of water. The edges of the figures are clearly delineated; only the wallpaper and the rug are painted in the more atmospheric style of the IMPRESSIONISTS. Cassatt had a remarkable ability to express an intimate connection between the figures in her work, particularly between adult women and children. Her work is clear and cool, with a flattened composition.

Cassatt found that her family was aghast that she wished to be a painter. She had a traditional art education in her hometown and moved to Paris against the wishes of those closest to her. She forged a strong friendship with the IMPRESSIONISTS and was connected to POST-IMPRESSIONIST Edgar Degas all her life. Her painter friends taught her how to achieve some freedom in her brushstrokes, but her work never entirely veered from the traditional. Cassatt was largely responsible for the Art Institute's fabulous Impressionist and Post-Impressionist work.

The first indication of an interest in natural light had appeared during the 17th century in the work of the Spanish court painter Diego Velázquez. In his paintings of ordinary people and even in his paintings for the court, he often replaced the dramatic, theatrical lighting of the BAROQUE with the softer, less predictable, ever-changing light of the real outdoors. Rembrandt, in his post-Baroque style, was obsessed with honesty in painting and sometimes used natural in place of theatrical Baroque lighting.

The only artists other than the Impressionists who had painted out of doors in France were the BARBIZON landscape painters. They were interested in capturing the accuracy of the landscape, so light was important only in the context of the overall picture.

▶    The label IMPRESSIONIST was attached to these painters by a cynical critic who was convinced they didn't know how to paint or draw and were capable of offering only an unfinished "impression" of the world. The critic took the word from the title of a Monet painting, **Impression, Sunrise** (1872). Both the people of the art world and those who knew nothing of art adopted the Impressionist label and sneered at these young artists. The Impressionists struggled financially, and it was only through the generosity of Caillebotte and Pissarro, both heirs to fortunes, that they survived the many years until they won respect. But money seemed unimportant to them because, as a part of art history, they were finally telling the truth about light and how it affected form.

As they grew older, most of the Impressionists became dissatisfied with the vagaries of real nature, longing for the studio and the imposed, balanced compositions they were taught to design as students. They returned to their studios, but their work retained the lessons of light, color, and the free manner of applying paint they had learned in their outdoor years. Only Monet remained a true Impressionist all his life.

From here, Post-Impressionism was born. Gustave Caillebotte, a friend and patron of the Impressionists but not an Impressionist himself, painted **Paris, A Rainy Day** (1877), seen in Gallery 201. Caillebotte was an engineer by education and profession, and his background shows in this huge canvas. His composition is architectural—if one figure were eliminated the design might collapse. Art students delight in "dissecting" this work with its repeating curves and rectangles. A true example of a place for everything and everything in its place, it becomes more human because of the shimmery, rainy-day light.

Seurat's *Sunday Afternoon on La Grande Jatte* has the logical organization of architecture.

One of the favorite paintings in the Art Institute collection is **Sunday Afternoon on La Grande Jatte** (1884), a work by Georges Seurat in Gonzales Hall, Gallery 240. Seurat was interested in the light and color of the IMPRESSION-ISTS but took an entirely different approach to them. His work is like architecture, with logically organized planes of space, poetically fixed forever in time. He imposes a RENAIS-SANCE-like perspective. His entire composition, with carefully controlled geometric forms, speaks of the Egyptian, CLASSIC GREEK, and ITALIAN RENAISSANCE but introduces some 19th-century elements such as flattened figures. The straight lines describing planes of space—the tree trunks, cane, and handles of the umbrellas—guide your eye back into space. The curves of the umbrellas, women's bustles, hips and hats, curve of the dogs' tails, monkey's back, and shadows all move the viewer rhythmically across the space. Seurat's primary interest, though, was color. He studied and furthered the color theory of the earlier 19th-century artist Delacroix, who had experimented with placing colors next to each other and allowing the viewer's eye to mix them. Seurat used dots of color next to each other throughout his paintings. It would take him a year or more to finish a canvas, but it didn't matter because he was fascinated with the concept and also felt that color mixed in the eye was clearer and purer than color mixed on a palette. A border completely enclosing *Sunday Afternoon* is also done in this method of painting, which is called DIVISIONISM or POINTILLISM. Seurat exquisitely combined shimmering light with a rigidly fixed mathematical composition.

Edgar Degas was one of the first people in France to own a camera. He was fascinated with this new technology and the ability to record one moment in time with his little black box. This "one moment in time" also became part of his paintings and drawings. Look at the painting **The Millinery Shop** (1882). The viewer catches the milliner unawares as she examines a hat. The hats in this asymmetrical composition are bright, large, and complex, but there is no question that the mousy-looking woman, dressed in drab brown, is the star of

"One moment in time": Degas's *The Millinery Shop*.

this moment. Degas was a master at composing a scene in which he directs your gaze to where he wants it to be. The tilt of the hats, the line of the table, and the hat in her hands form a frame for the milliner. Her lack of interest in the viewer makes her most interesting.

If the pastel **Dancers in the Wings** (1890) is in the gallery, note how natural the dancers are as they inhabit a scene that will never happen again in quite the same way. They are unself-consciously going about their business. Degas loved the ballet for its dramatic lighting and the contrast between the glamorous stage and the shabby backstage. He had a way of mixing pastels with something (probably oil), making the chalks look like particularly rich paint. Never in his lifetime did he tell anyone, not even Mary Cassatt, what his secret ingredient was.

Several bronze Degas sculptures, which are definitely products of that "one moment in time," are also in the museum. Often the figures are caught in awkward, clumsy moments, captured that way for posterity. In **Woman at Her Bath,** Degas shows a woman caught in a private moment that she probably would not have chosen to share with the world.

In **Bedroom at Arles** (1888), located in Gallery 241, Vincent van Gogh offers the viewer his refuge: his room. The perspective is tilted, as if to protect and cocoon the bed, but the odd perspective of the floor threatens to slide everything out of the picture. His depiction of space also helps to flatten the surface. The brilliance of the colors adds to the disorienting effect of the work. Van Gogh was one of the first artists in history to express his own, deepest, uncensored emotional responses on canvas, with his work flowing from the emotional problems he suffered all his life. His **Self Portrait** shows him looking worried, and he surrounds himself with short, jittery strokes of color that add to the tension in his face. Notice that he shows his face as ordinary-looking though he came from a family of handsome people who prided themselves on their looks.

Van Gogh's refuge: his *Bedroom at Arles.*

As an adult van Gogh spent time in sanitariums when he became too emotionally distressed to function effectively. He did not paint when he was in the throes of his depression, but after the "madness" lifted he was able to capture, with paint, the electric, pulsating feelings of the bad time. His ability and willingness to share his inner self was unique. Each stroke of his brush was an anxious portrait of his emotional state. His many psychological problems eventually led to his suicide in 1890. His works are always completely honest, originating from deep within his soul, and have short, sometimes swirling, and almost always nervous brushstrokes. The candid demonstration of feelings and fears in his work, and the use of brilliant color, often seemingly unrelated to the subject, subsequently influenced the work of the FAUVES, the German EXPRESSIONISTS, and the ABSTRACT EXPRESSIONISTS. (Paul Gauguin's early work, described in the pages to follow, shares the gallery with van Gogh.)

*At the Moulin Rouge* portrays the bohemian life that Toulouse-Lautrec knew best.

In Henri de Toulouse-Lautrec's **At the Moulin Rouge** (1892–1895), in Gallery 242, no one seems to be having a good time. The woman in the lower right corner is bathed in an acidic green light and seems particularly joyless. If you follow the orange hair of the woman at the table upward, you will see a self-portrait of the artist. He is the short-bearded man next to a taller, chinless man. Is this painting a commentary on the nightlife or on his life?

Lautrec was thrown from a horse as a small child, while showing off his prowess at jumping for his father's friend, and broke his thighs. He did not heal effectively, his legs never grew, and he lived in pain for the rest of his life. His wealthy, good-looking, aristocratic family encouraged him in his art and was not unhappy when he moved to Paris, away from the family estate where they didn't have to look at him. His early life fostered a cynical view of the world as shown in his paintings and prints. He flattened images and used bizarre color and lighting to express his skeptical worldview. Lautrec lived a bohemian life, spending most of his time in the nightclubs of the city where he drank himself into alcoholism and died young. Before his death in 1901, he created wonderful posters for his favorite nightclubs, using the performers who befriended him as models.

**Day of the God** (1894) by Paul Gauguin, located in Gallery 246, was painted in Tahiti. As the son of a French journalist and an aristocratic Peruvian mother, Gauguin had always deluded himself into believing he was descended from native tribes—a "noble savage" who had to protect himself from the excesses of the civilized world—so it seemed fitting that he would work on this tropical island. At first glance the large painting is primitive: simplified, flattened, carefree figures living an idyllic life from fetus through adulthood. The

Gauguin's *Day of the God* reflects his abstract sense of nature.

innocent natives are looked after by a god who is the central point of interest in the painting. Colors are arbitrary, especially in the amoeba-like, layered shapes of the lagoon. Like all his work, *Day of the God* is much more than the surface painting, deeper and more thoughtful than the scene itself. The work is about Gauguin's abstract sense of nature and its underlying forms as filtered through his sensibilities. It is also about how closely intertwined native people are with the land. He spent a great deal of time thinking of religion and believed that the tribal religions were closer to nature and thus to God. His musings on religion were abstract, and so was his art, despite recognizable forms. His most important artistic and philosophical idea was conceptual, and he encouraged artists who felt they had to paint something that existed in the real world to look at the object, throw something over it, and paint only what they felt about it. In spite of its primal subject matter, *Day of the God* is painted in a sophisticated, professional manner that speaks strongly of the artists's Western training.

Gauguin had been a successful banker and stockbroker with a wife and children before he began painting. Then he became friendly with the IMPRESSIONISTS, who taught him how to paint. He took up painting as a hobby but soon quit his job, went through all his money, and sent his wife and children to live with his in-laws so that he could become a full-time artist. The duality of his life as a middle-class husband and father while also a painter living a free, unfettered life, and as a civilized, educated Frenchman but also a noble savage, led to the duality in his painting. His figures were influenced by European styles, but he portrayed natives in an innocent setting. His life experiences and style were so integrated into his work that it becomes difficult to speak of one without the other. His style, called SYMBOLISM, strongly influenced Matisse and the FAUVES.

▶   At one point, when Gauguin found himself destitute, van Gogh—who greatly admired Gauguin's work—offered to share his room in Arles. Gauguin had no choice but to accept van Gogh's kindhearted offer. They painted together and learned from each other, but van Gogh's overwhelming admiration and charity irritated the testy Gauguin. Tensions eventually led to van Gogh cutting off his ear in frustration after an especially difficult quarrel. One of the important aspects of Gauguin's sojourn to Arles is that he left with an expanded knowledge of arbitrary color and emotional expression gleaned from van Gogh.

After leaving Arles he was able to find enough money to travel to "unspoiled Tahiti," where he did a fair amount to spoil his paradise by drinking to excess, marrying a 13-year-old Tahitian girl, and infecting some of the native population with syphilis. He was unbalanced in his life but brilliant in his work and his ideas.

Paul Cézanne may well be one of the most important painters in history. He changed the world's way of thinking and of looking. He led us into a fourth dimension of time before Einstein formulated the theory of relativity. His painting **The Basket of Apples** (1895), in Gallery 246, will show you the top, side, and bottom of the table, basket, ladyfingers, and as many viewpoints of the apples as there are apples. Cézanne thought, like Manet, that measured *perspective* had no place on a two-dimensional surface. Objects in the natural world do exist in three dimensions, and to paint them from only one dimension was a lie. Consequently he painted everything from various views: top, side, front, and back, making the viewer aware of space and the element of time as the artist moved around the model. Cézanne believed that everything in nature could be reduced to a cone, cylinder, or sphere, and each object in his work has a geometric base. In **The Bay of Marseilles** (1885), he layers the landscapes: buildings, water, and mountains, using cooler (blue and green) rather then greyed colors. Thus the viewer's eye moves back on planes of space without a measured perspective or the painterly lie that

Cezanne's *Basket of Apples* is one of his paintings that changed the world's way of thinking and looking.

colors actually become grey as they move back in space. The buildings are shown from the side, above, and below. In the portrait **Madame Cézanne in a Yellow Chair** (1888–1890), Cézanne allows the viewer to see the front view of his subject but also a semi-profile, the top of madame's head, a full and side view of her hands, and the top of her shoulder while offering a front view of the shoulder and chest. His paintings are carefully organized, with a strong underlying structure.

▶   An American painter, Erle Loran, spent several years dissecting Cézanne's work and making diagrams of many of his geometrically based, highly organized paintings. Loran's maps were published in *Cézanne's Compositions* in 1959. The Art Institute has an excellent collection of Cézanne's paintings. Paul Cézanne led the art world into the twentieth century.

▶ The 19th-century artists discussed in this tour moved away from the ideals of RENAISSANCE art and toward their own MODERNIST truths about the world they lived in. Through them, art of the twentieth century was able to change, adapting to the new world, new technologies, and new scientific theories and discoveries.

# TOUR 19

## The Art Institute of Chicago:
## Modernism: The Giants

---

Until the completion of the **Art Institute**'s new Modern Wing, the MODERNIST and CONTEMPORARY collections will remain in the older buildings. The works may be scattered, and you may have to find the collections by consulting a map, inquiring at the information desk, or asking a guard. You may not see the exact paintings or sculptures described, but the explanations of the styles and artists should help you enjoy the works on display.

MODERN ART encompasses the wildly creative work done between the beginning of the 20th century and 1945. It reflects artists' sensitivity to their changing times. Beginning in the 19th century and escalating in the 20th, social and technological change came rapidly and with dizzying consequences. Burgeoning ethnic populations competed for equality and attention; technology accelerated from simple industrial machines to complex electronics. Artists responded to some of these changes while searching for their own inner truths and their own brand of honesty in art. Many avant-garde artistic styles appeared in the early 20th century, so many that it became difficult to keep up with them. Finding acceptance for these expressions was even more difficult since they were outrageously different from what artists had produced before.

► The early-19th-century intellectual, writer, diplomat and ROMANTIC artist Eugène Delacroix observed that "Realism should be defined as the antithesis of art. The first of the Arts—Music—what does it imitate?" In fact there can be no reality in art.

The person, landscape, or object the artist translates
onto canvas, clay, or paper may be natural in appearance,
but only the actual model is real. The artwork becomes
a naturalistic interpretation. Artists from the 19th
century until today are not searching for objective
realism in their art but for an honest explanation
regarding some aspect of the world.

Pablo Picasso, the child of two artists, learned the basic
lessons of art and design at a very young age. Then he went
to Paris at age 17, explored painting in many different styles,
and yearned to find an important truth that would change the
direction of art and the way the world might be viewed. Picasso said he could draw like Raphael when he was seven,
which was true, and then he spent the rest of his life attempting to express the world as a child would. He worked in
many media besides paint—*collage*, bronze sculpture, *etchings*,
*lithographs*, and ceramics.

Picasso's **The Old Guitarist** (1903–1904) was one of his
earliest Parisian works, done in his early twenties, and part of
his Blue Period (1901–1904). It exhibits the despair felt by
this performer, an outcast of society whom Picasso befriended. It also shows the despair Picasso himself felt because his work was derivative and seemed to lack direction. In
the hands of a lesser artist, this painting could have become
maudlin, but Picasso simply reports the state of affairs.

In 1907 Picasso suddenly came to understand the philosophies of Cézanne: painting one view of anything was not
truthful. To be honest, one must show all sides of an object.
Following on Cézanne's belief that everything in nature
could be reduced to a basic geometric form, Picasso chose the
cube—as had the ancient Egyptians who had also wished to
show more than one view of the body in their paintings (see
pp. 122–124). In *Les Demoiselles d'Avignon* (at the Museum of
Modern Art in New York City) Picasso showed many views
of a cubed woman and, like Cézanne, he painted each view-
point independently of the others.

*Daniel-Henry Kahnweiler,* Picasso's fully resolved example of analytical cubism.

The work attracted the attention of a French painter, Georges Braque, and together Braque and Picasso invented ANALYTICAL CUBISM. Picasso's **Daniel-Henry Kahnweiler** (1910) is a fully resolved example of Analytical Cubism. The artist looked at a model or an object, reduced the observed forms to cubes, and walked around the model, painting each view simultaneously to capture the fourth dimension, time. (At about the same time Einstein was revealing his theory of relativity.) The face of the art dealer, Kahnweiler, is recognizable though fragmented. The appearance of fragmentation can be reconciled in the viewer's eye by picking out the top, side, and front views and reassembling them in his or her mind. The viewer must look more carefully to pick out different viewpoints of the shoulders, hands, and chest. Subdued earth *tones* combined with black and white cause color to become secondary and form primary. Picasso and Braque felt this to be a breakthrough in absolute honesty in painting and resented people who labeled their work AB-STRACTION.

**Man with a Pipe** (1915) is a SYNTHETIC CUBIST combination of painting and *collage* that was meant to answer the hated ABSTRACT label. Picasso and Braque invented Synthetic Cubism, which used geometric forms as a starting point, allowing the shapes to suggest objects or figures that were recognizable but not natural; instead they were invented. Since they were made up, form was less important, allowing distracting color and pattern to be brought into the mix. Parts of the face of *Man with a Pipe* vie for attention with the many patterns and colors in the piece. A vest sits low on the figure, and cartoonlike hands rest on the arms of a chair. Objects from the real world are glued onto the surface of paper or wood, with string for this piece, in hope that viewers will relate to the real materials and connect the articles to the truthful, natural world. By attaching objects, Picasso and Braque invented *collage*. How ironic: when they carefully observed what they were painting it was thought of as ABSTRACT, but when they made up objects and glued on arbitrary items, it was perceived as natural.

Picasso went on to paint in many more styles, using earth-mother figures and erotic images, and the monumental anti-war outcry of grief *Guernica* (at the Museo Nacional Centro de Arte Reina Sofia, Madrid). The classically painted **Mother and Child** (1921) portrays the solidity and protective qualities of women. Picasso presents earth women, simplified in form, who are overwhelmingly massive and protective, rocks tied forever to the land.

Henri Matisse's **Bathers by a River** (1913, 1916) includes four simplified figures in a lush landscape on the left, and then the work metamorphoses to the starkest of backgrounds, seeming to imitate day and night. Just slightly off center, a snake slithers onto or recedes from the canvas. Is it the good snake of the ancients on Crete or the malevolent snake from the Garden of Eden?

**Apples** (1916), a joyful still life, does not appear to be about apples but rather about circular forms against the rectangles of the table's pedestal and the rectangles forming the background (black on the left and across the top, golden on the right). The composition is rich with patterns of apples, of circular forms defining the plate, black lines, and obvious brushstrokes in the background, yet it conveys the impression of a minimal essence. A canvas more exuberantly patterned is **Lemons on a Pewter Plate** (1926). The wildly patterned red-and-white floral background, pink tablecloth, and yellow lemons could have produced discord but instead create excitement and unity.

To understand Matisse you must know that he was influenced by tribal art, the philosophies of Gauguin (see Tour 18), ISLAMIC ART, and Cézanne's concept of space, indicated through warm advancing and cool receding colors. Attempting to leave the Western tradition of optical illusion, he avoided *perspective* and experimented with seemingly arbitrary color as a symbol for feeling. Matisse's paintings are about emotion but also about line and the relationships of colors and patterns on a flat surface while implying three-dimensional space. His work vacillated between dense details, patterns, and utter simplicity. His late works were super simple: giant cutouts fashioned from brilliantly colored papers, expressing the *joie de vivre* that he always felt about art.

Matisse's group included Raoul Dufy, André Derain, Maurice de Vlaminck, Georges Braque (briefly), and the American Marsden Hartley. They were called FAUVES, or Wild Beasts, because of their seemingly arbitrary use of brilliant, excitable, bestial color.

Wassily Kandinsky was the first ABSTRACT EXPRESSIONIST. He sought to express—through colors and free, sweeping brushstrokes—the spirituality he felt so deeply. A Russian aristocrat, one of his earliest memories was of the brilliant

Matisse's paintings are about emotion but also about line and the relationships of colors and patterns on a flat surface, as in *Interior at Nice.*

colors of a Moscow sunset. He left the study of law to become a painter, hoping to capture the colors and rhythms of nature that were so important to him.

If **Improvisation with Green Center** (1913) is on display, you will see bold swatches of brilliant color, tempered with fine lines and small areas of detail. Observing the brushstrokes and the variation of line gives the viewer an entrée into the artist's psyche. **Improvisation No. 30** (1913) is an intoxicating whirl of color with intimations of cannons and wheels at the bottom of the canvas. Later in his life Kandinsky joined the BAUHAUS in Dessau, Germany, and his

*Improvisation with Green Center* by Kandinsky, the first abstract expressionist.

paintings began to emphasize a highly geometric, controlled inner self. An example of work done during his BAUHAUS years is **Untitled (Composition with Gray Background) (1941)**.

► Kandinsky was profoundly intellectual, writing deeply and at length about art. In his book *Concerning the Spiritual in Art* he speaks of art and music. In the translator's introduction, M. T. H. Sandler says, "Kandinsky is painting music. That is to say, he has broken down the barrier between music and painting, and has isolated the pure emotion which, for want of a better name, we call the artistic emotion." In Kandinsky's introduction he talks about the PRIMITIVES: "Like ourselves, these artists sought to express in their work only internal truths, renouncing in consequence all consideration of external form." Throughout the book Kandinsky seems to ask if our arm is more real than our inner feelings—just because you can pinch your arm, does that make it more real to you than an inner idea or inner pain?

The DADA movement planted the seed for the revolutionary art movement that is now called CONCEPTUAL. Dada grew out of the disillusionment that followed World War I, the first modern war fought with modern weapons, which destroyed people and values. A group of intellectual artists and writers declared that people who could inflict such atrocities upon other people were absurd, and that all their undertakings, including art, were equally absurd and worthy of mockery.

Marcel Duchamp used irony to express his own distaste for the world. He went to junk shops where he purchased discarded items: a urinal, a chocolate grinder, a bottle rack, for example. Duchamp's **Hat-Rack** (1915) is just that, a hat-rack found in a resale shop. It is meant to hang from a wall or ceiling, and when it does, it looks like a spider. Duchamp submitted found objects to art galleries, exhibits claiming that as an artist, if he deemed something art, it was. His pen-and-ink drawing **Nous Nous Cajolions** (1943) is of a woman who looks like a bride, holding a baby, and standing next to jail-type bars, partially hiding a figure.

Man Ray's **Percolator** (1917) is a painting of the filter basket inside a coffeemaker. The basket dominates the canvas and regurgitates coffee grounds. The colors are grey and umber, and the quick, sloppy manner of painting adds to the sense of a pot of coffee run amok. Man Ray, a photographer, used experimental means of photographic printing to make nontraditional statements and invented the *photogram*, originally called the "rayogram."

Kurt Schwitters created *collages* such as **Aerated VIII** and **MZ 13 Aufruf** (1919). Schwitters collected discarded papers and other trash from the street and formed them into carefully organized, neatly put-together *collages*. He made junk aesthetic. He collected so much trash—too much for collages—that the overflow filled an entire house. Eventually he filled three houses and called them *Merzbau*. He preserved them as works of DADA art, but they were all destroyed by bombs in World War II.

André Breton, a psychiatric hospital aid during World War I, saw the horrors the mind could produce when exposed to brutality. He believed in Freud and the possibilities of purging one's monsters by expressing the unconscious. He encouraged artists with an interest in Freud to call upon their innermost unconscious thoughts and, no matter how disconnected those thoughts seemed, to translate them into art.

Salvador Dalí painted monstrosities in deep landscapes, portraying the transformation and combination of objects, blood and decay, and fear of impotency. **Inventions of the Monsters** (1937) and **Visions of Eternity** (1936–1937) are two of his works in which dreams run amok and are used as fodder for analysis.

René Magritte's painting **Time Transfixed** (1938) is a painting of a traditional living room fireplace, but a train is emerging from where the fire should be. The artist created everyday situations and then inserted a bizarre element that makes the viewer see how close SURREALISM or the unconscious is to the commonplace.

In **The Policeman** (1925), Joan Miró's line is free and appears to be formed from *automatic writing* in a dreamlike scene. He presents a linear, partially painted horse rearing up on its hind legs as it faces a childlike policeman. In the savage **The Two Philosophers** (1936), Miró speaks of the brutality and senseless human behavior of the Spanish Civil War. Two hostile creatures creep toward each other, too self-absorbed to notice the ominous sky. His sculpture **Stone** looks like an ancient stele with slithering white lines.

Miró, an artist who always maintained a sense of a child's delight in the world, expressed a personal mythology in his innermost secret visions of nature. His paintings and sculptures are fun but also introduce intellectual subtleties and relationships of forms.

Balthus painted **La Patience** (1943), in which a prepubescent girl kneels on a chair in an opulent room. With teenage melancholy mirrored on her face, her emerging sexuality simmering, she seems to wait, but for what? Balthus was a master at depicting the disturbed, repressed, and ominous psychological characteristics of adolescent girls.

Marc Chagall invented forms, figures, and landscapes to populate the Russian, Yiddish folktales he heard all of his life. In **Birth** (1911–1912) a baby has been born and chaos exists in the hyper-brilliantly colored room. In **White Crucifixion** (1938), Christ is on the cross and people run away from him or cover their eyes. In **The Praying Jew** (1914), the figure wears the tallith and tefillin, paraphernalia of the Orthodox Jew, with one eye closed and the other open and very observant. Chagall's most famous pieces in Chicago are the **American Windows** (1977), large brilliantly colored windows filled with fantasies on a rich blue background. Ask a guard if it is being shown and where.

Chagall's *American Windows* are brilliantly colored and filled with fantasies.

André Breton wrote the *Surrealist Manifesto*, calling upon artists to create devices that allowed them to recall their dreams and to use free association. The results are dreamlike, invented images that don't always make immediate sense. The art requires the viewer to think or suspend rational thought altogether. The Art Institute of Chicago has a huge, excellent collection of SURREALISM.

Giorgio de Chirico, though not a Surrealist himself, provided an influence for the Surrealists. In **The Philosopher's Conquest** (1914) a classically composed landscape with a measured *perspective* is accompanied by cannon, cannon balls, and a tiny train. Two threatening, spiky artichokes act as guards with a message of "no entry," and the viewer is allowed to do no more than look. At first glance the balance and excellent craftsmanship make the painting appear logical, but on closer inspection it is irrational and dreamlike, the objects illogically placed in the setting. It describes a world of great loneliness.

The MINIMALIST Piet Mondrian looks easy, but he's not. Two of his Art Institute works are **Composition (No. 1) Gray-Red** (1935) and **Lozenge Composition with Yellow, Black, Blue, Red, and Gray** (1921). The *Lozenge* work is painted on a triangular-shaped canvas. In both these works Mondrian creates a rational world of squares and rectangles using only *primary colors*: red, yellow, and blue, with black the absence of all color and white the inclusion of all color. The formal elements of line, shape, and color are the subject matter, presented without distractions. He orders the world as the religion of theosophy, giving the world everything it needs to survive without frills. When humans added frills, they doubtlessly produced the troubles that beset humankind. At first glance the world seems cool, efficient, balanced, smooth, carefully measured, and removed from feelings. Look again— the squares and rectangles are asymmetrically balanced; Mondrian was a master at supposing how large and where each shape should be. His paint application shows very human brushstrokes, and some minor sloppiness has a sensual quality,

In *Composition (No. I) Gray-Red,* Mondrian creates a
rational world of squares and rectangles using only
primary colors.

giving the world everything it requires with nothing extraneous. Mondrian attracted some followers in a movement called
DE STIJL.

Paul Klee expressed nature and imagination as one. His
outer and inner worlds are harmonious. In **In the Magic
Mirror** (1934) two profiles, defined by one curving, moving
line, face each other; you see them only one at a time as each
gives way to the other. Two almost identical eyes express different feelings for each face, looking quizzical, optimistic,
and sad. The tiny heart, black and away from the interesting
faces, eventually becomes the center of interest. Klee was a
musician as well as an artist, and his work is always rhythmic.
Line is all important. There is always deeper meaning in his
work, looking for a viewer to unlock the door between the
earthly and the cosmic. The SURREALISTS tried to claim Paul

Klee as their own, but he insisted on working independently, without affiliations.

▶     Because of Klee's intellectual curiosity and thought processes, his fans have always looked for deep meaning in all his decisions. Chicago artist Walter Chruscinski asked Paul Weighart, a former student of Klee's, why Klee worked so small. Weighart, at the time a teacher at the School of the Art Institute of Chicago, answered, "Mr. Klee worked so small because Mr. Klee had a very small studio."

EXPRESSIONISM was influenced by the spontaneous, deeply emotional brushstrokes and colors of van Gogh and by the inner turmoil of Edvard Munch. German painters responded to their own inner screams before and especially after witnessing the horrors of World War I. Their work was emotional, sometimes hysterical, expressing highly personal feelings of fear, anxiety, and anger. During the Nazi reign in Germany, however, Hitler banned the Expressionists, calling their work decadent and anti-German.

Oskar Kokoschka produced painful portraits with psychological overtones. **Commerce Counselor Ebenstein** (1908) has a tortured, sad face, and the brushstrokes are vigorous, almost violent.

Max Beckmann's **Self-Portrait** (1937) shows him as imperious, but the fragmented background suggests that life is less than satisfactory. **Reclining Nude** (1929) is a figure that is beyond voluptuous. She reclines in a manner that is brash, crude, unsophisticated, and somehow hopeless. Beckmann's nightmarish paintings often featured doll-like people stuffed into small spaces, suffering the most horrendous violence.

MODERNIST sculptors featured at the Art Institute include Constantin Brancusi, Alexander Calder (see pp. 19, 20, 93, 132), and Henry Moore. Brancusi sculpted simple, unadorned shapes. His **Golden Bird** (1919–1920), one of 27 bird sculptures, is simple and elegant, with details that are only implied (the beak and tail). With one line, one sweep of

The details of Brancusi's *Golden Bird* are only implied.

material, he expressed what it took other artists multiple lines and shapes to say. The base for the perfectly polished bird is a contrast in less-finished wood. Brancusi said, "All my life, I have sought to render the essence of flight." An artist who understood the quintessential nature of his subject, he was a master craftsman whose highly finished, perfect surfaces draw viewers to want to touch his work.

▶   The old Museum of Modern Art in Paris reproduced Brancusi's studio complete with the chaotic mess he worked in. His gleaming, polished, pared down sculptures rising from the tumultuous litter never looked more beautiful, more resolved.

Henry Moore's work feels massive and monumental, even when it's small. In his semi-ABSTRACT **Reclining Figure** (1957), the upper part of the body and head are small with *negative spaces* allowing the outside world in. The bottom section is massive, and an egg shape is cradled between two large shapes representing the legs. His themes of extreme simplicity, respect for materials, and integration of negative and *positive space* create a dignity and oneness with the environment. His work emanates a solid stability, a sense that the figure has been in that place since time immemorial.

If Joseph Cornell's **Boxes** are on display, plan to spend a little time and a lot of attention on them. They are marvelous small stage settings expressing what the artist saw and imagined what he saw during brief glimpses into strangers' homes while riding the elevated trains (now defunct) in New York City. Look beyond the theatrical aspects and behind the scenes in these SURREAL, EXPRESSIONIST works.

MODERN ART at the Art Institute of Chicago will take you an hour. If you have time, you may continue on to view the CONTEMPORARY ART section described in the next tour. If you are out of time, consider the next section as a separate one-hour tour.

# TOUR 20

## The Art Institute of Chicago: Contemporary Art

---

After DADA it becomes clear that nothing in art is certain, the rules must be rewritten. Artists, like scientists, have always stretched themselves to think, explore, reinterpret, and remake their world. In EARLY CHRISTIAN and continuing with MEDIEVAL ART, artists struggled to find a way to educate an illiterate population in the tenets and salvation of Christianity without using images that were presumptuous enough to copy what God had created. They communicated through figures of arbitrary proportions and non-naturalistic flat space, making everything symbolic. GOTHIC artists came to presume that they were given the ability to copy what God had done, so why shouldn't they? This way of thinking led the Gothic Giotto and the 15th-century ITALIAN RENAISSANCE artists who followed Giotto to attempt naturalistic figures and a scientifically perfect mathematical *perspective*.

Artists of the 19th century also responded to social and technological change by rewriting the rules of art and developing an interest in scientific concerns—light, color, space, and time. Artists of the early 20th century took those ideas further, and the later 20th- and 21st-century artists let loose their ideas that dealt purely with the mind or technology. These CONTEMPORARY artists continue to rethink and refashion the world. This tour covers the styles and artists that will most likely be seen in the Contemporary section of the new MODERN Wing of the **Art Institute.**

Jackson Pollock, an ABSTRACT EXPRESSIONIST painter, laid his large, unstretched canvases on the floor so that he could walk around and in them, becoming one with the work. In **Greyed Rainbow** (1953), his dripped, poured, and brushed

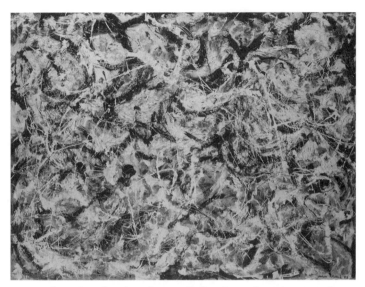

Seemingly undisciplined, Jackson Pollock's *Greyed Rainbow* is in fact coherent, unified, and controlled.

paint may seem undisciplined, but his many years of traditional painting while studying and working with regionalist landscape painter Thomas Hart Benton made the compositions coherent, unified, and controlled. The viewer can follow the rhythms of Pollock's work that are much like the underlying rhythms of nature he painted daily with Benton, created by the bold black, grey, and white brushstrokes, the moving white strings of paint that come forward, and the glimpses of fresh oranges, yellows, and blues lying under the surface. The considerable skills he developed while painting with Benton remained within him as he created ABSTRACT records of his own inner psyche. Pollock's line is as physical, nervous, and frenzied as he himself was, his work becoming a frantic autobiography. He was brilliant but self-destructive, given both to drinking and driving too fast, resulting in his death in 1956 from an automobile accident.

Willem de Kooning was also classically trained and greatly influenced by the ITALIAN RENAISSANCE as well as by

CUBISTS and SURREALISTS. In his totally nonobjective **Excavation** (1950), the primarily white surface (though yellowed slightly with age) is punctuated with red, blue, and an orangy yellow. Black lines that suggest *automatic writing* slice and slither in, out, and around the white. The surface is rich, painterly, and highly personal. De Kooning's work is usually nonfigurative, but you can often glimpse a distorted, ambiguous figure or object. He created a series of erratic, energetic, and erotic **Women**, with ABSTRACTED, misshapen, Rubenesque figures violated by the world. De Kooning always offers shifting perspectives, wildly violent brushstrokes, and brilliant, arbitrary color. His paintings consist of the instantaneous application of paint that is revised after the initial emotion is expressed. He considered himself a craftsman, and the control of the paint and compositions in his work exemplify this. The viewer is in the presence of the artist's deepest feelings but also of his intellectual, rational improvements.

Franz Kline, an ABSTRACT EXPRESSIONIST, simplified and broke down forms to their most essential elements. In **Painting** (1952), great swatches of black rush across the canvas while verticals try to slow down the horizontal movement. It feels like a collision of energetic forces. The work looks as if it had been done quickly, but that's not true—Kline did many sketches before beginning a canvas. After he expressed his initial feelings, he adjusted and readjusted to achieve maximum impact. He vented his emotions through slashing paint strokes of black and umber on a white background. When he did add color, it was quite beautiful but never seemed necessary. His deeply felt, tense work was about structure and line, and though he never rendered a deep space, the viewer can always see what comes forward and what goes back.

In Clyfford Still's **Painting 1958** the intensely dark paint covering the canvas changes in *tone* from cool to warm, creating shifting space. Textures vary, and a vertical white line just off center teases the viewer—is it coming from beneath, or is it on the surface? A small orange brushstroke at the bottom definitely comes from a world behind the dark surface.

Still presents large, gestural, freely painted canvases that are MINIMAL expressions but not totally minimal. Like Mark Rothko (see Tour 16), his expressions are simple but too emotionally charged to be fully minimalist. They are flat but hint at a mysterious space through the manner in which color is applied and layered. Sophisticated in composition, use of color, and texture, they also exude a primitive vitality.

Cy Twombly, an American artist who lives in Rome, creates a style of ABSTRACT EXPRESSIONISM that seems to unravel Pollock's forms, making them larger, looser, and more like *graffiti*. In **The First Part of the Return from Parnassus** (1961) the artist uses less-traditional writing and more *automatic writing*. Like a drawing, this canvas offers an intimate view of the artist's hand movements: something like reading a person's unconscious doodling. Twombly is highly literate and well versed in the classics, and he uses shades and *tones* in mysterious ways, both of which make every mark on his canvas appear to come from deep within. The fragments of cursive writing in the work provide clues to ancient myths, poetry, and personal narratives. At first glance his scholarly understanding of early civilizations contrasts with the obsessive graffiti used by adolescents to seek attention. Upon further investigation it becomes an intellectualized form of populist wall scribbles. The writing gives unity to the painting by producing rhythms and tensions across the surface.

Ellsworth Kelly is the ultimate MINIMALIST. **Red Yellow Blue White and Black** (1953) is sure to be on display. In this painting the black panel is in the center, the other colors fan out from it. Blue, the cool, recessive color, is placed on either end. Look carefully at each piece separately and observe what happens to the color, what your eye sees when you look at the space above or below the color. The painting represents the possibility of every color in the world if you mixed only the *primary colors* or added black or white. Very often the wall behind the canvas will reflect the *complementary color*: red will reflect green, yellow reflecting violet, and blue reflecting orange. The large, pure canvases change the space by causing a personal response to each color or noncolor. In essence your eye is the artist as it sees reflections and changes in the simple colors. Kelly was classically educated, painted in a representational style, did *collages*, and seemed headed in a SURREALIST direction. Eventually his interests centered on patterns, shadows, and the nature of *negative spaces*. His interest in the individuality of color led to the canvases that best represent him, each one smoothly painted in one hue with no modulations. Color alone is the subject matter, and each canvas with color is unique.

Gerhard Richter, one of Germany's most famous artists, works in a wide variety of styles. One example of his work is

In *Woman Descending the Staircase,* Gerhard Richter joins the natural and the imagination.

seen in **Woman Descending the Staircase** (1965), which was influenced by Duchamp's 1912 *Nude Descending a Staircase (No. 2)*. In this style Richter begins with a photograph, attempting to keep the look of the photograph but blurring or smudging areas with paint, maintaining but disrupting the original image. Here is a joining of the natural and the imagination, and you learn to distrust your first reaction to the work. His ABSTRACT work also blurs and scrapes away surfaces to reveal mysterious under layers.

Sol LeWitt, MINIMALIST sculptor and pioneer in CONCEPTUAL ART, was an artist within a mathematician (or vice versa). His original works, such as **Nine Part Modular Cube** (1970), made of baked enamel on aluminum, are pristinely white, three-dimensional square frames, modules placed together to form a greater square. As the viewer looks at, into, and around the grid, squares intersect each other, creating smaller squares and shadows; light changes to tonal *values*; and there is always something new to look at. Simplicity

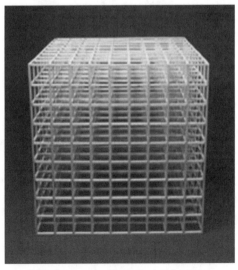

Simplicity forms complexities in Sol LeWitt's
*Nine Part Modular Cube.*

forming complexities becomes the theme, and cold geometry takes on a warm, inviting look. Later he moved even further into CONCEPTUAL ART. Another LeWitt that you will probably see at the Art Institute is a wall drawing done from a set of his instructions and optional diagrams for making large, mathematically based, pencil murals. As lines are drawn per instruction, they change a bit from the originals either because of the site or because human beings are wont to make subtle changes no matter what guidelines they are following. LeWitt becomes the composer of these works, and the person translating becomes the tool for playing the composer's composition.

Eva Hesse's **Hang-Up** (1966) is an artist's stretcher frame covered in subtly toned rope, each area another *tone*. An absurd (Hesse's word) thin metal rod aggressively reaches from the frame into the environment. Ironically, her artistic inse-

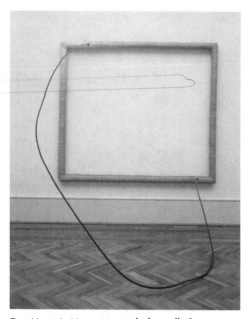

Eva Hesse's *Hang-Up* might be called romantic minimalism.

curities and fears that her paintings were empty and failed to reach anyone seem to be inherent in the empty frame: escape into the world is made possible by the rod. Hesse was a German Jewish child of the Holocaust, a girl whose mother committed suicide. She dealt with her insecurities, depressions, and fears through psychoanalysis, but they continued to plague her. Confidence in her work alternated with feelings of inadequacy. She died of a brain tumor at the age of 34, leaving behind a multitude of truly beautiful drawings and deeply emotional three-dimensional sculptures in atypical media: latex, fiberglass, cheesecloth, rope, and wire. Her work entwines the emotional and the intellectual. Her most important work might be called ROMANTIC MINIMALISM, using only the essence of a feeling and idea but creating it from offbeat materials that bear the artist's personal mark. Hesse's work was an early foray into the CONCEPTUAL.

Carl Andre is another MINIMALIST/CONCEPTUAL artist. His work, **Steel Aluminum Plain** (1969), alternates light and dark squares of steel laid together on the floor. The viewer becomes part of this dark, light, smooth, and cold part of the environment—step on it, hop over it, sit on it, and as your stance changes, so does the environment. If the squares remain on the floor they are art, if they are taken apart each square may be used for something else. The world holds infinite possibilities for change.

Now look at what seems to be the polar opposite of the Minimal/Conceptual style: the POP art of Roy Lichtenstein, Jasper Johns, and Andy Warhol. The POP artists, fearful that ABSTRACT art appealed to the elite and would crowd out OBJECTIVE ART altogether, returned to the use of images. The images they chose were popular icons easily recognizable by all, and often part of commercial art and advertising. Their work and the objects they chose to paint were often thought crass. Perhaps that is what they were meant to be—like DADA, challenging the views of the art elite.

Roy Lichtenstein's **Brushstroke with Spatter** (1966) and **Mirror in Six Panels** (1971)—broken pieces of an ABSTRACT design are reflected continuously across six panels—are both from Lichtenstein's abstract period. The Lichtenstein paintings that most people are familiar with have cartoon characters and banal subject matter, flat figures heavily outlined in black, and balloons saying what the characters are thinking—comic-book style. Raised on comics, Lichtenstein adopted this format in his art, becoming both OBJECTIVE and abstract. Newspapers and comic books are printed on cheap paper, and the color is laid on in tiny dot patterns that capture the ink. Lichtenstein enlarged and painted these dots in all his paintings. In his objective work he told the public what the cartoons were about and what he thought the public was being told to value by advertising agencies. In his abstract art he painted what might be backgrounds, settings for his earlier figures, displaying the essences of place.

Jasper Johns most likely will be represented by **Corpse and Mirror II** (1974–1975), a painting of various panels, each painted separately, each a variation of the others. The title *Corpse* is derived from "exquisite corpse," a game played by SURREALISTS to trigger unconscious thoughts. To play Exquisite Corpse, a paper would be folded and each artist assigned part of an object or figure to draw. When the artist finished drawing, he would fold the paper so that it couldn't be seen, and the next artist would draw whatever part he or she was assigned. When everyone finished, the paper was unfolded and a weird, dreamlike drawing revealed. Johns appears to have been playing that game with himself in this work. Also shown might be **Near the Lagoon** (2002–2003), an *encaustic* painting in *tones* of blue with hinges and string attached. Johns used various popular images, including letters, numbers, and the American flag, showing them in a context different from what would be expected.

Andy Warhol's depiction of **Mao** (1973) should be on display. Warhol used POP icons that were being sold to the public at that time—Mao Zedong, Marilyn Monroe, and the Campbell's Tomato Soup can, for example. He planned the work and hired untrained people to *silk-screen* the colors onto the photographic images. The silk-screeners were not taught to line up the screens carefully in order to assure that colors went on exactly where they were meant to be. The consequences, as can be seen in *Mao*, were sloppy edges and colors where they shouldn't be, revealing the lack of craftsmanship so prevalent in the 20th century. Because Warhol did not do the actual work, he spoke of the disconnection of modern people from their own worlds. Warhol, a successful advertising executive, left his position to do silk screens, using advertising's modus operandi: forcing you to remember the product by repeating it over and over again. He emphasized how society manipulated people to buy, buy, buy, see, see, see. Ironically, shortly before his death, Warhol began to do easel painting, enjoyed it enormously, and valued the craftsmanship in his newfound media.

Bruce Nauman has worked in various styles and media—sculpture, photography, neon, video, drawing, and performance—to create obscure but provocative and often political messages. **Clown Torture** (1987) is a video installation. **Diamond Africa with Chair Turned D,E,A,D,** (1981) consists of great steel beams forming a diamond shape. Cables keep the shape aloft at the viewer's eye level, where it assaults the person looking at it. An overturned chair hanging from a beam could be a person hanging. The work refers to the economic oppression of diamond workers in South Africa and might also refer to that country's previous apartheid. Nauman is interested in communication and often uses words presented in flashing neon lights to grab your attention, making you think about what the words mean.

Martin Puryear's sculpture **Sanctuary 1982** combines two graceful branches on a wheel that supports an exquisitely fashioned box. The artist adores and respects nature and natural phenomena. He is interested in the duality of nature and embraces opposing forces, always thinking in terms of flexibility. Working with diverse forms, he shows respect for his materials and is not threatened by combining different types, such as wood with rope, or wood with tar on wire mesh or rawhide. Puryear adds subtle details that make the viewer consider other possibilities. His sculpture is powerful, mysterious, often massive despite its fragile elements, and sometimes it is even aggressive. The work balances mobility with stability, permanence with ongoing time. Like nature, the artist never completely refines his work.

The Art Institute has a substantial collection of CHICAGO IMAGIST artwork, including Jim Nutt, Karl Wirsum, and Ed Paschke. Nutt and Wirsum were members of the 1960s Hairy Who group and Paschke a part of the False Image group. The Hairy Who group also included Gladys Nilsson, who used "hairy" images that were busily intertwined, and painted tacky subjects in luscious colors; Art Green, who layered strange, hard-edged shapes to express deep space; Suellen Rocca (see p. 132); and James Falconer, whose harsh, disrupted, anxious figures expressed an irreverent, often sexually charged view of the world gleaned from cheap ads. This group spoke of subject matters that had never before been exposed artistically: underwear, mucous, armpits, and hemorrhoids, for example. Their craftsmanship is as superb as their subject matter is seedy. They were heirs to the earlier Chicago artists called the MONSTER ROSTERS. Art historian Franz Schulze described the work of the Hairy Whos as having "an acrid strength, admittedly crude but fierce, a powerful albeit dog-eared kind of art that was the equivalent of rock music and specifically a Midwest type: lonely, flat, hot, bawdy, intense." Chicago's False Image group, of which Paschke was a member, espoused views similar to the Hairy Who group. Both groups began their careers at the Hyde Park Art Center where they were given space for showing and promoted by artist Don Baum (see pp. 115, 223–224).

Like a MEDIEVAL painter, Jim Nutt elegantly builds up his layers of paint until the colors glow. In **Miss E. Knows** (1967) he recreates the body by breaking it down and redesigning it in a somewhat vulgar, clumsy manner. This expressive and important take on the world reminds the viewer that life is sometimes beautiful but often tense, unattractive,

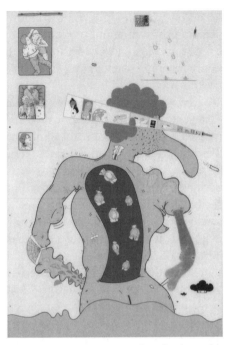

In *Miss E. Knows*, Jim Nutt breaks down the body and redesigns it.

even gross, and art speaks of the world, gorgeous or not. The redheaded *Miss E.* is a sexually ambiguous figure. It appears that her back is to the audience, but are those bulges at each side breasts or muscles? Is that a small, perky breast materializing from behind the back? Her nose is penis-shaped, and she has the beginnings of a beard. A thin triangular form pierces through her head and comes out of her eye, indicating her hyper vision. Are those her thoughts pictured on the triangle? Another penis shape rises on her back and is filled with a pattern of buttocks. In the top right corner is a small rectangle depicting violence. *Miss E. Knows* is painted on both sides of a piece of Plexiglas. The other side of the painting is a bright green door that is tightly closed. *Miss E. Knows*, but what does she know? Does she know the secrets behind the door? Is it a door or boarded windows or the top of a closed box? Do the words and numbers hint at what it is and what it contains? Life's mysteries, the things that we all would like to know but can't put our finger on, seem to be the subject of this painting.

Karl Wirsum's **Screamin' Jay Hawkins** (1968) offers a surface that is brilliant in color and obsessive in pattern, much like the Mexican FOLK ART that influenced Wirsum. The main figure is painted on a flat surface but looks as if it were constructed piece by piece and could stand free of its background. The figure is covered in a variety of shapes that read like a *mosaic*. Each separate part of the body is clearly defined, appearing as though it were hinged and could move independently of every other part, making you wonder if the figure is the ground or the ground is the figure—it takes time to discern the spatial places. A strange halo of light in knife-like points encompasses the head and body that, along with bolts of lightning inside the figure, gives the work an electrical surge. Two birds at the top of the design seem to be screaming at each other. In this broad, unconventional approach to art, Wirsum uses words to connect the viewer to the real world. Your eye keeps moving to take in the design, space, and visual puns of his work. If a painting could talk, Wirsum's would scream.

Ed Paschke's **Minnie** (1974) is from his **Showgirl** series of the 1970s. The colors are acidic, brash, and loud. The exaggerated female figure is distorted and the face somewhat masculine though heavily made up. Paschke used overall body tattoos on many of the *Showgirl* bodies. He boldly faced social and cultural issues in his work, using the crude images of cheap magazines and the raw urban environment. When he was in school at the Art Institute of Chicago, he frequented theme bars inhabited by people on the fringes of society, such as bikers and transvestites. Although his work sometimes looks as if it were airbrushed, Paschke was a magnificent craftsman and achieved that look through the meticulous use of myriad small brushes. His work can intimate vi-

Acidic, brash, and loud: Ed Paschke's *Minnie*.

olence, appear combative, and often speaks of voyeurism. He portrayed boxers and American-type gangsters; later, some of his imagery imitated electronic technology.

Another important CONTEMPORARY artist featured at the Art Institute is Felix Gonzalez-Torres. The *entablature* atop the arches on the Michigan Ave. façade of the Art Institute building inscribes the name of historically important artists, an idea Gonzalez-Torres used in **Untitled** (1989), a running text at the top of a room, just below the ceiling. He immortalized important societal dates along with dates meaningful to him personally. He continued to add dates until his untimely death in 1996. The work is unassuming, quiet, and calls for reflection. Each time the *Untitled* work is installed, the owner of the piece is obligated to add or subtract dates so that the work remains pertinent. Gonzalez-Torres's life is perpetuated each time *Untitled* is seen.

Cindy Sherman is a CONCEPTUAL photographer. The Art Institute has a series of **Untitled** photographs that mimic the shape of *Playboy* magazine centerfolds. It is about the stereotyping of women as vulnerable victims. Sherman always photographs herself in costume, imagining herself (and the viewer imagining her) in a multitude of roles. In many cases her self-portraits point out the stereotypical roles women are supposed to play in society.

Born in Japan, On Kawara travels the world painting dates. In all his work, including **October 31, 1978**, Kawara carefully prepares a ground with several layers of a smoothly applied color, sanding between each layer of paint until the surface is perfect. He applies the monochromatic color without gradation. He then carefully paints the date, such as *October 31, 1978*, by hand. That date and whatever implications the viewer brings to it become the theme of the work. In some of his work Kawara adds a subtitle, quote, or thought. If the work is not finished by midnight of that date, it is destroyed. He places each painting in a box with newspapers published the day of the painting. The backgrounds of different dates may look alike, but they aren't because he mixes only enough color for one canvas. The next batch of paint may be close to the original but is never exactly the same.

Did you ever imagine adding your own touches to an established work of art? In **After Egon Schiele** (1982) you see 18 photographs of 18 different paintings by the EXPRESSIONIST painter Egon Schiele. Sherrie Levine takes photographs of other people's photographs and paintings to express something different. The question remains whether Levine's photographs are valid as works of art.

In the paintings by Robert Ryman, **The Elliot Room Charter I-V** (1985–1987), paint becomes the theme. Using only white on four matte surfaces divided by horizontal bands, Ryman makes the paint itself, the very personal brushstrokes, and the surrounding environment the subject matter. He paints on canvas or metal sheets using the most neutral of colors, white. Each of the pieces is a different size, and every one is held by four fasteners placed at different locations on the individual surfaces. The work calls for contemplation and concentration in order to discern the subtle differences. It is rigid in its execution but speaks of freedom of choice within a very limited experience.

For more 21st-century art, see Tour 22 of the Museum of Contemporary Art.

# TOUR 21

## The Art Institute of Chicago: American Art

---

The American Collection at the **Art Institute** may be seen in the Rice Building, where a small sampling of artists' work is displayed.

Georgia O'Keeffe attended the School of the Art Institute of Chicago, and the museum has a large collection of her work. She created a group of **Cloud** paintings at a time when she was frequently flying between New Mexico and New York while settling her husband Alfred Stieglitz's estate. The Art Institute has one of the outstanding paintings in the *Cloud* series, **Sky Above Clouds** (1965), a large atmospheric representation of the heavens, an observation from above the earth. Another O'Keeffe in the collection is **Black Cross, New Mexico** (1929), influenced by the scenery of her home in the Southwest. A flat cross, with varying shades of black, stands boldly at the front of a canvas with majestic mountains and a multihued sky behind. O'Keeffe combines objects in simplified, flat compositions that are based on natural forms yet ABSTRACT in nature. Her landscapes are about the atmosphere, her flowers about the essence (the reproductive possibilities) of the bloom.

Grant Wood, a Regionalist painter, was also a student at the School of the Art Institute. His famous **American Gothic** (1930) portrays a somber, hardworking, and stern Midwestern farm couple with their GOTHIC church behind them. The models for this painting were Wood's sister and his dentist. The design of the work is a classic lesson in composition: how the oval shape is repeated in the faces, the brooch at the woman's neckline, and the window of the house; how the pitchfork shape is repeated on the front of the man's overalls and a plant on the porch. Wood remained true to his small-town Midwestern upbringing, and his work reflects the values of small-town America. He was influenced by earlier FLEMISH paintings, from whence he derived his excellent craftsmanship.

Edward Hopper's **Nighthawks** (1942) is a classically painted scene showing the interior of a diner at night. Despite four people present in the diner, each one seems totally alone, with actual and psychological space separating them. Hopper used geometrically based compositions, clear-edged forms, and dramatically shadowed interiors to show isolation and loneliness in a transient America.

Winslow Homer observed his surroundings and painted them. His interest in light led him to the sea and the people who made their living from the sea. The **Coast of Maine** (1893) is a painting of a violent sea crashing into the coastline. The **Herring Net** (1885) shows two large fishermen working in bitterly cold, damp weather in front of a misty sea.

The most influential works of painter Charles Demuth were of CUBIST shapes interspersed with letters and numbers, such as in the painting, . . . **And the Home of the Brave** (1931). In **Spring** (1921) Demuth paints 12 overlapped, rectangular samples of fabric that look like *trompe l'oeil*. The paintings used many symbols, some of which were based on poems.

Ivan Albright, a Chicagoan much of his life and a graduate of the School of the Art Institute of Chicago, is probably best known for his **Portrait of Dorian Gray** (1943–1944), painted for the movie of Oscar Wilde's story. *Dorian Gray* and Albright's other paintings are merciless in their depiction of the corruption of the soul shown through the disintegration of the body. His work is obsessively detailed, beautifully painted, and often difficult to look at. In **That Which I Should Have Done I Did Not Do** (1931–1941) he paints a decaying door, the jamb bowed and appearing too decrepit to stand much longer. On the door is a funeral wreath, and a delicate hand reaches out to the wreath from the left side. **Into the World**

**Came a Soul Called Ida** (1929–1930) is a portrait of a woman well beyond her prime, with a ruined face and cellulite-infested legs. Hope springs eternal as she sits primping at her dressing table filled with brushes and potions.

The Art Institute is a world-class museum with great collections from many different cultures and peoples. The outstanding Asian collection has treasures from China, India, Japan (with a wonderful collection of *woodblock prints*), Southwest Asia, and the Near and Middle East. There is a small but very interesting collection from Africa, primarily from West and Central Africa but also including a smaller group of sculptures from East and South Africa.

If you have an Art Institute of Chicago membership, you can make an appointment with the print and drawing section to view the work of an artist of your choice. You will be given white gloves to wear and what looks like a Popsicle stick for turning pages, and you can spend an hour or two with Rembrandt, Degas, Cézanne, and others. This department has an amazingly rich collection of prints and drawings.

# TOUR 22

## The Museum of Contemporary Art

To reach the Museum of Contemporary Art, at
220 E. Chicago Ave., turn east on Chicago Ave.
from N. Michigan Ave. and walk a block to the
front entrance of the museum. If you are driving,
turn west from N. Lake Shore Dr. onto Chicago
Ave. The map for Tour 10 shows you the location
of the museum. There is a parking garage on
Chicago Ave. at the far east side of the museum
building. Be sure to have the museum stamp your
parking ticket for a reduced fee.

► A visit to this museum is a treat for those who enjoy
or are curious about current art, but it's not easy for
those who haven't been initiated into the mysteries of
CONTEMPORARY ART. **The Museum of Contemporary
Art (MCA)** has exhibits that change every few months,
but it does not regularly show its permanent collection.
Thus CONTEMPORARY ART cannot be explained by work
that is always on display at the museum. Instead, see
Tour 20, where art after MODERNISM (after 1945) is
explained in a manner that will cover the general
direction, philosophy, and reasoning of contemporary
work. This tour will further discuss CONCEPTUAL ART,
so often featured at the Museum of Contemporary Art.
After reading the explanations, you can approach shows
at the MCA and draw your own informed conclusions.

Some years ago a Chicago artist, Paula Manaster Stein, went
to a new dentist. As he examined her teeth, he remarked that
he had heard she was an artist but certainly hoped she didn't

do any of that modern stuff. When Paula was able to speak again, she remarked that she knew he was a dentist but certainly hoped he didn't use any of that modern equipment.

Since no one knows what art will become historically significant, see as much new art as possible and draw your own conclusions. Because art defines its own time, it also defines the people of that time—including you.

Historically, each era has produced art that speaks of the social, economic, religious, scientific, and technological aspects of the artist's time. Even as far back as the era of cave paintings, artists used their technology: painting, drawing, and magic to address their concerns about having enough food, keeping themselves safe from predatory humans or animals, and reproducing. Their wall paintings were probably about magically capturing the spirits of the carefully observed and drawn animals they most needed for food and clothing. They may have thought that if the animal's spirit were elsewhere, it might not fight back so vigorously.

As Sol LeWitt once wrote, "In CONCEPTUAL ART, the idea, the concept is the most important aspect of the work. When an artist uses a conceptual form of art it means that all of the planning and decisions are made beforehand and the execution is a perfunctory affair. The idea becomes a machine that makes the art." In other words, the new art is about the intellectual process rather than the concrete product. In this age of photography, film, video, and computers, we are bombarded with images. The Conceptual artist wants to make the image less important but the need to think more important. John Cage, composer, philosopher, writer, and printmaker, believed that "the idea, the concept, the process, not the finished product was the most important thing about art." Looking at new ideas in art can be intellectually stimulating—and fun—once you let go of the idea that art must look a certain way in order to be art.

The MCA says its mission is "to be an innovative and compelling center of CONTEMPORARY ART where the public can directly experience the work and ideas of living artists, understanding the historical, social and cultural context of the art of our time. The museum boldly interweaves exhibitions, performances, collections and educational programs to excite, challenge and illuminate our visitors and to provide insight into the creative process."

▶ Before you enter or when you leave the museum, please take time to look at the building itself. In the 1990s the museum's board commissioned German architect Josef Paul Kleihues to build a new museum larger than the museum's old home on Ontario St. (formerly a bakery). The front entrance moves you across a plaza and up a granite outdoor staircase to a glass entryway. (If you need an entrance without stairs, you'll find an elevator at the north end of the building.) The walls surrounding the front doors are built of rectangular, dark grey aluminum panels fastened in place by stainless steel bolts. The effect is classical in proportion but heavy and aggressive in appearance. It is not in harmony with the site that features graceful residential buildings on the north, GOTHIC structures of the Northwestern Medical Center complex to the south, and Lake Michigan to the east. Many people feel threatened rather than welcomed by the entry. Once inside the museum, the lobby and the galleries are large, bright, and inviting. It is a great place to exhibit and view art without distractions. Different from the entrance on the west, the museum wall facing east is filled with light and expansive, with a large glass wall that softens the metal panels. Outside are terraces with a view of gardens and the lake.

Shows that the Museum of Contemporary Art has presented in the near past include: Lee Bontecou, Kerry James Marshall, Massive Change: The Future of Global Design, and Rudolf Stingel. With descriptions of the art shown in these exhibits, you will be able to discern what the MCA finds important to bring to its audiences.

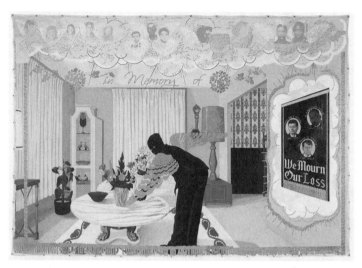

The large canvases and somewhat flattened black figures of Kerry
James Marshall are part of his effort to document the African-
American experience through the portrayal of daily chores.

In 2003 the museum offered the work of Kerry James
Marshall, a Chicago artist and recipient of the coveted
MacArthur Fellow Award, in the show **Kerry James Marshall: One True Thing, Meditations on Black Aesthetics**.
Marshall's experiences as an African American make him feel
that it is his social responsibility to document the African-
American experience, confront civil rights issues, and show
black history. His large canvases with somewhat flattened
black figures and sharply defined edges are placed in three-
dimensional settings. The figures display all of the possibilities of the human experience as people go about daily chores,
taking care of their world.

In 2004 the museum presented **Lee Bontecou, A Retro-
spective**. Bontecou has worked in various styles and has been
influenced by tribal art, the very sophisticated sculptor Brancusi, bones, and machines that express engineering genius
while at the same time causing violent destruction and war.
As a counterpoint, Bontecou's work always has an underlying

structure: nature. She has stretched canvas over metal frames to create *constructions* with dark holes that seem to suck the viewer in. Those pieces, her most widely known, speak of war and sex. The fabric is stitched together, giving an overall sense of being tattered and tired. On closer inspection, the excellent craftsmanship is apparent, and the viewer becomes aware that the sloppy, worn-out impression is part of the message. Bontecou's drawings are magnificent and the *chiaroscuro* masterful. In many drawings she uses soot instead of charcoal, creating the darkest of darks. From the 1970s and into the 21st century, she has used vacuum-formed plastics to make fish and strange flowers that are delicate but maintain a sense of threat. She integrates anger against war alongside the beauty of the natural world. She uses multiple materials and intricate details, and makes all the diverse elements work together.

In 2006 **Massive Change: The Future of Global Design** prompted viewers to do a double take—what was this show doing in an art museum? Produced by designer Bruce Mau, its purpose was to show how to use technology to design everything in the world in a way that would pose less of a threat to society. The show crossed disciplinary boundaries, demonstrating how everything and everyone is interconnected, making all people accountable to all other people. Design, it declared, is an integral part of art and has the power to change life. A brochure designed for the show explained, "It's not about the world of design. It's about the design of the world." The approach relates closely to the early-20th-century BAUHAUS theory of making the world a better place through art and design.

**Rudolf Stingel**, a one-man show at the museum in 2007, presented the ideas of the artist about the idea of painting. Stingel approaches the long-posed questions: What is painting? Is painting dead? His conceptual questions aim to make you rethink your perceptions of painting. In his exhibition, people were invited to become part of the environment, a piece of the painting. An orange carpet left to become dirty by the repeated footsteps of the foot traffic changed the visual response to orange and carpet. Aluminum foil stretched on the walls of the lobby and corridors of the museum encouraged visitors to write, draw, gouge the surface, and change the optical sense of the walls. Footprints forced into the soft surface of Styrofoam created a multileveled impression on what was once a smooth surface. Stingel attempts to demystify all art and make you a participant in the reconfiguration. His paintings are atmospheric in the tradition of Monet or Rothko: the Styrofoam with footprints is as adoringly composed as a painting would be. As you viewed the "paintings," it became apparent through his emotional brushstrokes and use of color that Stingel loves to paint. In Francesco Bonami's book about Stingel, he writes, "Stingel's impressions left by the pattern of fabric or the soles of boots are the same as the impression left by the subject on the canvas."

The Museum of Contemporary Art has a rich permanent collection that is too large to be listed in its entirety but includes the artists Vito Acconci, Francis Bacon, Lee Bontecou (see pp. 200–201), Alexander Calder (see pp. 20, 93, 132), Christo, Donald Judd, René Magritte (see p. 171), Bruce Nauman (see p. 187), Claes Oldenburg, Robert Rauschenberg, Robert Smithson, Andy Warhol (see pp. 185, 186–187), and H. C. Westerman, all from 1945 to the 1970s. From the 1980s and 1990s the museum has collected Magdalena Abakanowicz (see pp. 50, 52, 131), Chris Burden, Chuck Close, Jenny Holzer, Anselm Kiefer (see p. 127), Jeff Koons, Jim Nutt (see pp. 188–190), Martin Puryear (see pp. 187–188), Cindy Sherman (see p. 192), Lorna Simpson, and Thomas Struth. The most current artists represented in the collections are Matthew Barney, Andreas Gursky, Arturo Herrera, Jim Hodges, Judy Ledgerwood, Kerry James Marshall (see p. 200), Catherine Opie, Rudolf Stingel (see pp. 201–202), Sara Sze, Kara Walker, and Jeff Wall. A few of the artists in the collection are discussed here to give the reader a sense of what type of art is collected by the museum.

Vito Acconci is an architect and PERFORMANCE and IN-STALLATION artist. **Convertible Clam Shelter** (1990) is what it says it is—a very large open clamshell, made of fiberglass, clamshells, steel, rope, light, and sound. It is shiny, seductive, and exhibits the potential to snap closed unexpectedly. Beware! Acconci's work is often confrontational and sometimes documents his provocative, offbeat fantasies.

The English painter Francis Bacon is an EXPRESSIONIST whose work features screaming anguish, shock, and violence. In **Study for a Portrait** (1949) an unhappy, resigned figure is trapped in a glass booth, on display much like an animal in a zoo. Bacon has said about his work that "it unlocks deeper possibilities of sensation."

Christo and his wife Jean Claude wrap everything they can lay their hands on and get permission to envelop. In **Orange Store Front** (1964–1965) they keep the viewer from seeing what is behind the windows, subverting what store windows are designed for. In the past the couple wrapped the entire Museum of Contemporary Art when it was in its former home on Ontario St. They swaddled small islands off the coast of Miami Beach in Florida. They ran a curtain along the Pacific Coast in California. They built 753 saffron-colored fabric gates throughout Central Park in New York City, and they swathed Berlin's Reichstag. Of Bulgarian descent, Christo grew up in this Iron Curtain country where everything was hushed for fear the Soviet police would not like what was being said. Is it that he, accompanied by Jean Claude, still expresses that historically important, secretive side of the world? The wrapping is temporary, a conceptual refiguring of the area that is re-clothed. The work takes what appears to be simple and reminds you of the complexity inherent in everything.

One of Donald Judd's pieces in the MCA collection is **Untitled**, a work fashioned from plywood. Judd reduces his expression to the simplest shape, repeating it, making its proportions and relationships, as well as the overall relationship of the shapes to their environment, the subject matter of his work. Wanting the duplicated shapes to be autonomous, with no personal connection to the artist, Judd does the mathematical calculations and contracts with a craftsman to build the pieces. The forms are flawless, emotionally removed from everything but the essence of itself. When installed, the work articulates the space by its placement and the shadows it creates.

Robert Smithson was labeled an Earth artist. His largest piece was **Spiral Jetty**, built in 1970 on the Great Salt Lake in Utah. When he spoke of his work, his language suggested that he thought of it as an expanded method of painting. A film of the *Spiral Jetty* is owned by the MCA. Formerly a painter, Smithson found large areas of uninhabited land, received permission from the land owners, and, using heavy equipment, dug or built designs that can be seen from above. His work changes the environment without harming the land.

Robert Rauschenberg creates what he calls *combines* or *assemblages*, using the detritus of modern life with an ABSTRACT EXPRESSIONIST's sensibility. **Retroactive II** (1963) prominently displays a photograph of John F. Kennedy amidst a plethora of everyday images that invade all of Rauschenberg's pieces. The many elements look chaotic but take on a unity through shape, color, and line. Shockingly enough, his most influential teacher was Josef Albers, the most MINIMAL, mathematically based of artists (see pp. 128–129). In spite of the minimal influence, Rauschenberg produces very busy, large-scale works using painting, *collage*, and often actual three-dimensional objects (for example, a stuffed ram, a quilt, or a pillow) on or alongside the canvases. His work is often about complexity and constant change in contemporary life. In an early film of Rauschenberg's studio, a small, seemingly ignored television set is shown flickering. The unrelenting, instant changing of reflections on the television apparently influenced Rauschenberg and reflects the differing, simultaneous visions in his work.

H. C. Westerman, originally a Chicago artist, attended the School of the Art Institute. **Billy Penn** (1976), made of sheet metal, steel, wood, and bronze, takes its title from the name stamped on the pipes that he used in the *construction*. His small, SURREAL worlds are ambiguous in meaning, often funny, magical, and wildly imaginative. Westerman, a great craftsman, is influenced by his fantasies, his reactions to his wartime encounters, and the excesses of modern society. His works are thoughtful, but they are also meant to amuse and please.

The MCA has **The Other Vietnam Memorial** (1991) by Chris Burden, a highly controversial artist, in its permanent collection. The *Memorial* has rectangles fanning out from a central core, and lists every service man or woman killed in Vietnam. Burden's work is aware of and attuned to the dangerous social and political aspects of the world. In 1975 he began to make installations, including one that used war toys to create a connection between the powerful and the military. The artist, whose resumé includes a doctorate and a professorship at the University of California at Irvine, confronts his audience and makes them often unwilling participants in his art. The dangerous tone of his art emerged early in his career. In the 1970s the public was invited to the Museum of Contemporary Art to view a performance by Burden. The setting featured a glass panel, a clock, and a hammer. The artist entered the gallery and immediately lay down on the floor, where he remained without moving. Hours passed; confused, people began to leave. After a very long time, museum officials became worried that something was wrong or that remaining in one position might damage Burden's internal organs. In spite of a contract stating that the museum would not interfere with his performance, they called the paramedics. As soon as medical help arrived, Burden rose, picked up the hammer, smashed the clock, and left, threatening to sue the museum for breaking the contract. At another performance, people waited in a gallery until he and a friend entered, standing quietly at opposite ends of the room. Some time elapsed, then suddenly his friend shot him in the leg. He shocked—and continues to shock—the art world out of its complacency with tradition.

Chuck Close painted a portrait of **Cindy** (1988) in his style of taking photographs of people, putting them on a grid, and then marking a huge canvas with a grid that conforms to the one on the photo. Close copies each square of the photo onto the corresponding square of the canvas, creating a gigantic painting. He sometimes varies the images by using a variety of styles; for example, he may shift the grid, producing a broken, cubistic image. In 1988 Close was stricken with an illness that left him a quadriplegic, but he did not allow his disability to keep him from his studio. At first he painted by holding the brush in his mouth, but after regaining some movement, he had the brush strapped to one arm. He continues to paint in that manner (Renoir painted the same way when, late in life, arthritis crippled his hands).

Jeff Koons's work is reputed to be the most expensive among all living artists. A factory produces his Neo-POP art. Works in the MCA collection are **Three Ball Total Equilibrium Tank** (1985), three basketballs suspended in what looks like a fish tank, and **Pink Panther** (1988), a porcelain figure of a glitzy, sexy, bare-breasted woman with a pink panther slung over her shoulder. Koons uses the most banal images, and much of his work is *kitsch*; but he receives commissions around the world. One of his three-dimensional works that may seem familiar is the gigantic West Highland Terrier covered in growing plants and flowers. The "green" dog is called *Puppy* and lives in several locations, including outside the Guggenheim Museum in Bilbao, Spain. Is Koons warning us that we are sliding into an ignorance of what is truly beautiful and what is shallow glitz? Is he telling us that education is unimportant because whatever we like is art? Perhaps his work is an important description of what society is becoming. Or is he a charlatan?

Judy Ledgerwood's gorgeous paintings are large and speckled with large dots and circles. **Driving into Delirium**

(1995) is made from oil and wax (which repels oil). You can lose yourself in her glowing work and instinctively feel how much she loves to paint.

Photographer Catherine Opie originally specialized in portraits but since 1997 has been photographing American cities, expressing the psychological presence of its communities. Her architectural images are in black and white, but when she photographs the moods of **Lake Michigan** (2004–2005) at different times of the year, she presents them in color. Opie's architectural work is quiet, devoid of people, capturing the specific identity of each city and neighborhood.

The *chromogenic* development print **Cremaster 2: The Drone's Cell** (1999) and the three-dimensional **Cabinet of Frank Gilmore** (1999) by Matthew Barney are important parts of the museum's collection. All of Barney's work is SUR-REAL, a highly personal combination of his own life and some secret story. The exploration of the human body is important in what he does and gives his work an underlying erotic quality. Barney, considered by some to be one of today's most important young artists, fuses video, photography, *installations*, sculpture, and drawing. His installations often recall PER-FORMANCE ART.

Thomas Struth presents huge photographs taken in art museums or at historic sites, about visitors looking at the art and architecture. The museum owns Struth's **Milan Cathedral** (1998) and **Todai-Ji, Daibutsu-den, Nara** (1996). The audiences in his photographs vary from enthralled to interested to distracted to disinterested. Struth has said, "I felt a need to make these museum photographs because many works of art, created out of particular historical circumstances, have now become mere fetishes, like athletes or celebrities, and the inspiration for them is fully obliterated."

The museum often has shows that include work from its permanent collection. You may visit at a time when you can see some of the work described above. Whatever show you come upon when you visit the Museum of Contemporary

Art, you are sure to be titillated and come away with questions that will draw you back.

If you are mentally and physically weary after an exciting, thought-provoking hour of MCA exhibits, you can rest while having an elegant sit-down lunch at Wolfgang Puck's restaurant on the main floor at the east end of the museum, or pick up a quick snack at the southeast end of the large, glassed-in restaurant area. In summer you can sit outside on the terrace, enjoying the gardens and glimpses of Lake Michigan. On Tuesday evenings in the summer, Puck offers a limited menu of appetizers, salads, and drinks to enjoy while you listen to live jazz.

The Museum of Contemporary Art is open on Tuesday 10 a.m. to 8 p.m., and Wednesday through Sunday 10 a.m. to 5 p.m. It is closed on Mondays and on Thanksgiving, Christmas, and New Year's Day. Suggested admission is $10, $6 for students with IDs and seniors, and is free for children under 12 and military personnel. Tuesday is free for everyone. The bookstore carries a rich selection of books as well as unique jewelry and other gifts.

# TOUR 23

## The National Museum of Mexican Art and Pilsen's Murals

From the Loop, take the Pink Line or the Blue Line El destined for 54th and Cermak. Get off at the 18th St. stop and walk west to S. Wood St. Turn left (south) to W. 19th St. and to the museum at 1852 W. 19th St. You will travel from the museum to the murals in this neighborhood afterward.

TOUR 23

ON TOUR

1 Paintings, mosaics at El station
2 National Museum of Mexican Art
3 Orozco Community Academy
4 1805 S. Bishop St.
5 Casa Aztlán
6 1900 S. Carpenter St.
7 Murals on R.R. embankment
8 Painting/collage (Monopoly game references)

ALSO OF INTEREST

A 1260 S. Laflin St.

► The Mexican Museum was founded in 1982 and was renamed the **National Museum of Mexican Art** in December 2006. Since its inception, its mission has been "to stimulate and preserve knowledge and appreciation of Mexican culture through sponsoring events and exhibitions that exemplify the rich variety of visual and performing arts in the Mexican culture; to develop a significant permanent collection of Mexican art; to encourage the professional development of Mexican artists; and to offer arts education programs."

The National Museum of Mexican Art at 1852 W. 19th St. is free to the public with the exception of an occasional fee for a special exhibit. The hours are Tuesday through Sunday 10 a.m. to 5 p.m. It is closed on Mondays and major federal holidays.

The museum, a remodeled boathouse, is a delight to look at with its brightly colored interior walls. One gallery is devoted to rotating shows and another to the work of Chicago's Mexican artists. As always, if you have more than an hour, look at whatever catches your fancy, particularly the ancient artifacts shown in glass cases. For the hour tour you will visit the gallery for the museum's rich permanent collection. Excellent explanatory signs accompany the artwork.

The first few rooms are called "Our Past Is Present." As you enter you will see a painting of the **Virgin** by Miguel Cabrera (1740–1768). The Virgin's body is a flattened image with layers of cloth and no hint of what is beneath the fabric in European MEDIEVAL style. Her face, with its shadows indicating the three-dimensional world, is more reminiscent of the European late-GOTHIC style.

In a glass case to your left is an engraved gourd called **From Corn Dough to My Child—My Body Is for You** (2005) by Olegario Hernandez. The gourd is incised with graceful design and figures. The figures are shadowed to indicate they occupy three-dimensional space. Also in this space note the clay **Fertility Figures.** The small, cone-shaped breasts are so different from the short-legged, huge breasted, and large-stomached *fertility figures* found in prehistoric Austria. They have more in common with the slender, elegant fertility figures of a pre-GREEK culture, the Cycladic Islands.

A large painting that at first glance appears to be embroidery because of its small, stitchlike strokes is the work of Mario Castillo. Called **Las Memorias Antiguas de la Raza del Maguey Aun Respiran,** or **The Ancient Memories of Mayahuel's People Still Present** (1996), the media is acrylic paint mixed with the semen of the artist. Castillo explains in the description of the work that "the painting would contain an extraction of [his] 'body presence.'" Spend a bit of time clearing your mind while concentrating on the work and you will be able to see the colors transform themselves into an ABSTRACT field of energy.

A long, horizontal work looks like an old painting on stone. It appears to be weather-beaten. On closer inspection it is an oil painting on canvas done in 1927 by Jean Charlot and called **Chichén Itzá Relief**. Although nothing rises from the surface (*relief*), the *chiaroscuro* is handled masterfully, giving the impression that the band at the top projects out. The figures are blocky, the shapes reminiscent of Mexican mural painting.

In a glass case in the room marked as the "Mexican Colonial" section, you'll see a 17th-century **Baby Jesus**. His face is that of a teenager with some of the baby fat remaining. His baby's body has the confident stance of a man. It is possible that the artist, attempting to show the wisdom of Jesus, could not simply represent a helpless baby, instead infusing his image with a thinking face and a confident carriage.

A glowing golden altar entitled **Retalbo** (2001), by Alejandro García, has brightly painted images of the miracle and life of Christ with Mary and the patron saints. If you aren't careful, you can spend the better part of the hour looking at the many images on the altar. In the same room is a fabulous

*Retalbo*, a glowing golden altar by
Alejandro García.

painted cross, **Untitled**, made of dried reeds and varnished
wood by Luis Guillermo Olay Barrientes in 2002.

At the far end of the room is a large painting, **Battle at
Puebla** (1987) by Alejandro Romero. Showing horses advancing at a furious pace, the painting achieves its energy
from the wildly generated paint strokes behind the horses. A
group of what seems to be secular figures at the bottom left
crowd together, and a similar section of church-type figures
mass at the bottom right. Are they avoiding troubles gallop-
ing toward them?

The next room is labeled "Post Mexican Revolution to
Today." As you enter, look to the right for three Diego Rivera
drawings. Thoughts of Rivera as a tough, self-confident, aggressive painter of bold shapes are bent here as you see another aspect of him. The sensitivity of line in these drawings,
such as in **Sin Título** (1949), speaks to another side of his
character.

The **Day of the Dead** altars, ceramics, skeletal figures, monsters, and masks are all spectacular. Note the seriousness and the humor in these works. The Day of the Dead is a Mexican tradition that dates back 3,000 years before the Spaniards invaded the land we now call Mexico. This ancient Aztec ritual about remembering and honoring the dead and symbolizing death and rebirth is one that the Spaniards tried to stop in their attempt to convert the natives to Catholicism, but to no avail. They finally incorporated Day of the Dead rites into the Mexicans' Catholic theology. Skulls are worn and displayed, altars built, and parties and parades organized to embrace the twins of duality, life and death.

In a green room to the side you'll find iconic paintings and a red pickup truck with photographs of Mexican immigrants. A video of Mexican activist César Chávez is also part of the exhibit.

Three paintings of the **Lady of Guadalupe**, Mexico's most revered image, by Yolanda M. Lopez were done in 1978. The painting on the right is of a tough-looking young woman wearing tennis shoes and carrying what appears to be a knife in one hand and a snake in the other. She is draped in a heavenly blue robe. The second *Lady* has a knife and some fabric. The third is a self-portrait of the artist sewing. The *Lady* series ends with **Mona Lupe** (1975) by César Augusto Martínez. It is the Mexican take on Leonardo da Vinci's **Mona Lisa** and will end your tour of the permanent collection with a smile. Please be aware that there are more than 6,000 works of art in the permanent collection; there may be changes in the galleries at any time. The museum has an excellent gift shop.

From the National Museum of Mexican Art you can explore the rest of the Pilsen neighborhood to see its display of art out of doors. Many Chicago neighborhoods are rich in murals; for the most part, they depict the culture of a less-than-mainstream people or they are a cry for justice from those same people. Murals are often done in collaboration with the painter and community and become a source of pride for the area. The murals of Pilsen, a primarily Mexican community, are influenced by the Mexican revolutionary masters: Diego Rivera, José Orozco, and David Alfaro Siqueiros. The Mexican murals, whether done by the masters in Mexico or by their heirs in Chicago, tell of the pain and joy of ordinary Hispanic and Latino people. The shapes are often large and simple, the people heavy, solid forms.

If you came to Pilsen on the El, you have already seen that the surfaces of the El station at the 18th St. stop (where you exited the train) are covered with brilliantly colored Mexican and pre-Colombian designs. A variety of artists, including Francisco Mendoza, Joy Anderson, and many young people from the area created this painting that speaks of Hispanic culture and the fabric of the Pilsen neighborhood. The opulent painting is crowned by the *mosaic* entry to the station, also created by Mendoza and young volunteers.

One block south of the El stop at 1940 W. 18th St., the **Orozco Community Academy** is covered with splendid *mosaics* also done by Mendoza and students. The themes include depictions of the Mexican painter Frida Kahlo and local artists, as well as featuring sports and art themes.

Walk east on W. 18th St. toward S. Laflin St. and continue one block to S. Bishop St. At **1805 S. Bishop St.**, muralist Hector Duarte, a student of Siqueiros, led a group of artists in the painting entitled **Alto al Desplazamiento (Stop Gentrification in Pilsen)**. Employing Siqueiros's dynamic symmetry and varied perspectives, the artist shows worried, angry people who face intimidation and threats of loss of work from authority figures. The artists who worked with Duarte were connected to Chicago's Taller Mestizarte print workshop: José Guerrero, Jesus Gonzales, Luis Montenegro, José Pino, and Mariah de Forest. Duarte's mural showed the fears of people attempting to hold onto their homes and jobs when faced by high-powered developers and city politicians.

Again take W. 18th St. to S. Racine Ave. to the **Casa Aztlán**, 1831 S. Racine St., a community center where a fire in 1974 damaged many murals. Marcos Rayas, Salvador Vega, Aurelia Diaz, Carlos Barrera, and other artists reworked the outside walls with portraits of political and cultural heroes and neighborhood residents.

Walk south on S. Racine St. to W. 19th St., and then one block east to **1900 S. Carpenter St.** The mural is bright, colorful, and uses the building's actual windows as part of the painting. The color red is dominant as workingmen build and repair while two men appear to be holding a painted window that turns out to be the building's real window.

Walk north on Carpenter St. to 18th St., then turn west to Paulina, where you can take the El back to the Loop. To continue the tour, walk west on 18th St. to Racine, then walk north. At 16th St. between S. Racine St. and S. Blue Island Ave., Aurelio Diaz directed community members in painting block after block of murals on the wall of the railroad embankment. These murals show the diverse but similar heritages of Hispanics and Latinos. One of the paintings shows bold, overlapping profiles: the many faces of a contemporary Chicano.

Also at S. 16th St. and S. Blue Island Ave. is an amusing painting/*collage* about the gentrification fears of the Mexican-American community. Featured in the mural are residents backed up by a Monopoly game with elegantly dressed Monopoly figures, picturing how American bankers aggressively change the world with their (Monopoly) money.

If you are feeling energetic, take Racine St. six blocks north to S. 12th St. and then three blocks west to S. Laflin St. At 1260 S. Laflin St. a mural entitled **A la Esperanza (To Hope)** on the east wall of the Benito Juarez High School refers to local problems and encourages education. It was designed by Jaime Longoria and Malu Ortego y Alberro, who were joined in the actual painting by Marcos Raya, Salvador Vega, Oscar Moya, José González, and Roberto Valadez.

As you walk or drive the streets in Pilsen, you will see many more murals. This tour covers about a bit more than an hour's worth of looking.

▶    If you are interested in murals throughout the city, see the book *Urban Art Chicago* by Olivia Gude and Jeff Huebner.

# TOUR 24

## Illinois Institute of Technology

From the Loop, take the Green Line El south and get off at 35th St., the Bronzeville-IIT stop.

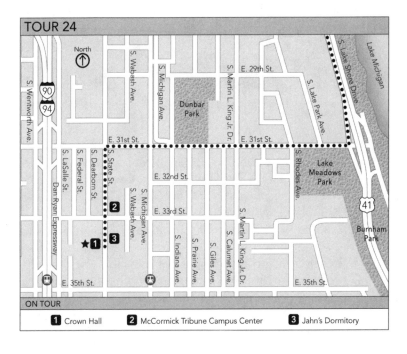

TOUR 24

ON TOUR

**1** Crown Hall     **2** McCormick Tribune Campus Center     **3** Jahn's Dormitory

Chicago has many college campuses, some with beautiful grounds and others of concrete. The campus at the **Illinois Institute of Technology** is somewhat controversial and certainly unusual. IIT (originally the Armour Institute) brought several artists, such as Laszlo Moholy-Nagy and Mies van der Rohe, to IIT from the BAUHAUS, the design school in Dessau, Germany, that was declared un-German and closed by Hitler

Crown Hall at IIT is a true example of Mies's "less is more" philosophy.

in the 1930s. Moholy-Nagy became director of the IIT design school; Mies headed the architecture school, also designing 20 buildings on the IIT campus. **Crown Hall** at 3360 S. State St., completed in 1956, the Mies building that houses the School of Architecture and formerly the Institute of Design, is one of his gems. (The Institute of Design is now at 350 N. LaSalle St.)

Rising from a concrete base that somehow gives the illusion of being lightweight, the glass building floats in space but gives the viewer a sense of stability because of the steel *columns* that occasionally stripe the glass. The roof hangs from four steel girders. Inside, the space is fluid, a single room without interior *columns*, the flexibility allowing changes in space as the occupant's needs change. The perfection of the proportions and the materials are the only decoration the building needs—a true example of Mies's "less is more" philosophy.

In the late 1990s the school, feeling the need to move into the 21st century, sponsored a design competition for a campus center directly across from Crown Hall. The winner was a high-profile Dutch architect, Rem Koolhaas. The site for the center was next to and beneath the very noisy elevated tracks. Koolhaas also designed a "silencer" (described below) for the El trains.

One of the problems facing Koolhaas was that Mies's **Common Building** would abut his new building at the northeast corner. Koolhaas, an admirer of Mies, did not ignore or do damage to the Mies building. As you look at the Mies building from the new building, it has not been ravaged physically or emotionally.

The new center, called the **McCormick Tribune Campus Center,** is a low one-story building, much like one Mies would design, but the similarities end there. It is difficult to get a full view of the building, and you may find yourself standing in the street and looking at the Campus Center in pieces. At the top, beneath the roof, is a dreadful non-*cornice*. It is a flat band (it doesn't project over the building) with black and red stripes. It doesn't seem to relate to anything else in the building. The glassy exterior bodes well for an

Rem Koolhaas's Campus Center attempts to complement Mies's Crown Hall.

open, light interior—indeed, the interior is much more attractive. But before you enter, look at the flattened stainless steel tube that surrounds the El tracks. This is pure theater. It is covered in corrugated steel, and when the Campus Center moves beneath the tube, it looks as though the El wraparound is resting heavily on the building's roof. It does muffle the noise and is fascinating to see. While the combination of the Campus Center and the tube is exciting and new, it feels unrelated to the rest of the campus.

Inside, the Campus Center is delightful: one huge space (but with *columns*) that, like Crown Hall, can be transformed according to the occupant's needs. Koolhaas directs what is to happen and where it is to happen by presenting brilliant color defining specified areas. (For example, red walls denote the computer center.) A sense of vitality comes from many people doing many things. Strolling through the Campus Center, you may sometimes feel that the building is not quite finished, but you aren't sure what makes you feel that way. The

The corrugated steel tube surrounding the El tracks is pure theater.

Campus Center contains places for studying or just sitting. It has many computers, a dining area, and faculty space. There is a delightful, amusing glass wall with likenesses of IIT leaders, including Mies. Note the little scenes that make up the leaders' faces. There is a somewhat DECONSTRUCTIVIST space where the ceiling is open and you can see the corrugated El tube peeking into the Campus Center. This building and the tube seem antithetical to the engineering emphasis of IIT, but they do offer a bit of humanization on a very mathematically oriented campus.

South of the Campus Center is Helmut Jahn's new **Dormitory**, which Jahn has said looks like a train. Three separate buildings are divided by three landscaped courtyards. The buildings are made of poured concrete and covered by corrugated stainless steel, strongly relating to the El tube. The main courtyard gate has walls and a roof of glass, the glass specially designed to reduce the noise of the El. Jahn did not wish to completely eliminate the El tracks visually or aurally because the El is a part of the experience of the IIT campus. He used concrete and glass to make the noise less invasive.

Jahn was adamant about using only absolutely necessary materials, without frills: the floors remain uncovered concrete, and the beams are exposed rather than finished. Jahn also designed the furniture for the rooms and apartments. The simplicity of the dormitories creates a sense of the new while still relating to Crown Hall and the other Mies buildings. Helmut Jahn, who had been a graduate student at IIT, seems to understand its culture and campus, providing a bridge between the "cool" Koolhaas, the gritty urban site of the school, and the school's older architecture.

▶     An interesting footnote about IIT is that its Institute of Design was the first school in the nation to offer a Ph.D. in design.

# TOUR 25

## Superior-Huron and
## West Loop Art Districts

For the Superior-Huron tour, take the #66 bus at
Chicago Ave. and Michigan Ave., going west.
Get off on Wells. Or you can walk the seven
blocks west on Chicago Ave.

For the West Loop tour, you may take the X20,
Washington/Madison express from Madison St.
and Michigan Ave. west to Morgan St., walk
four blocks north to 400 N. Morgan St., and
after you see the Dawson Gallery begin your
journey south.

Several neighborhoods in Chicago are distinctly "art areas"
in that a number of galleries are within close proximity. Two
of these areas are Superior-Huron (called River North) and
the West Loop. Here we describe several of the galleries and
a few of the artists represented by them.

The Superior-Huron art district spills over to N. Wells
St. where you will find the **Roy Boyd Gallery** at 739 N.
Wells St. Boyd Gallery features high-quality artists from the
United States and Europe. Most of the works are ABSTRACT,
but some are OBJECTIVE, such as those of William Conger, a
Chicago artist whose semi-abstract landscapes usually have
sharply delineated edges, giving them a geometric feel. They
look a bit like puzzles, and some of the puzzle pieces are
pointed and threatening. Brilliant in color, each piece uses
symbols that refer to the place where Conger is painting. In
recent years he has worked a great deal with *collage*. Roland
Ginzel, who is primarily a painter and printmaker, also does

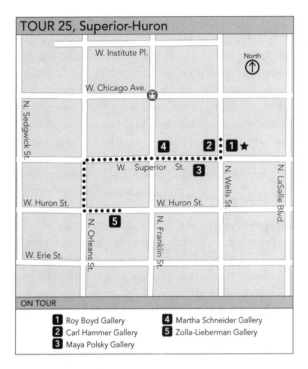

sculpture. Although at first glance his abstract work appears organic, it does have a geometric structure. Frank Piatek's subject is rounded tubes, with the tubes implying depth as they interlace like *medieval illuminated manuscript* designs. They are filled with sensual light, graceful movement, and are highly erotic. Teo González creates MINIMALIST canvases with monochromatic colors topped by many circular forms in patterns. This obsessive work has the perception of depth and movement, making you feel dizzy.

**Carl Hammer Gallery** at 740 N. Wells St. is unusual in that it houses very sophisticated artists, such as Chicagoan Hollis Sigler, an MFA graduate from the School of the Art Institute, who chose to return to primitive roots painting in a *naive* style. Her delicious colors and confident brush-strokes give her sophistication away. Don Baum, whose imagination is limitless, works in a SURREAL style. His earlier works were strange *constructions* filled with whole and parts of baby dolls. He is now doing beautifully painted scenes on boxes that look like birdhouses. IMAGIST Phyllis Bramson uses ordinary objects in extraordinary settings to create playful pieces. She often addresses the connections between men and women. Hammer Gallery also represents many *naive*, untutored artists such as Henry Darger, a janitor who never gave any indication that he did artwork but left a treasure trove of paintings and drawings when he died. His landlord, a well-known Chicago photographer, Nathan Lerner, discovered the work when he was cleaning Darger's apartment. Darger illustrated his fantasy stories, such as **In the Realms of the Unreal**, with figures of children fighting child slavery and the winged, horned beings that were their enemy. The work is about young girls and has frightening violent and erotic undertones. Lee Godie used to sell her work along with her sarcasm on the front stairs of the Art Institute. Godie attracted many customers, including artists and art students. Her work is flat, linear, and simplistic. Mr. Imagination had a vision after he was shot and almost killed. The vision, accompanied by a voice, told him that he was to be an artist. His work consists of carved sandstone, thrones, discarded bottle caps used to form figures, and paintbrushes that are decorated to represent heads and many other imaginative phenomena. Joseph Yoakum started painting in his seventies and attempted to portray the world as it appeared to him. As his work progressed, it became his vision of the places he said he had visited or hoped to see—his inner fantasies were probably based on what he wished he had done.

Around the corner at **Maya Polsky,** 215 W. Superior St., you can see CHICAGO IMAGIST Ed Paschke (see pp. 190–191); Jose Cobo, a Spanish, three-dimensional artist who does installations, figures on stilt legs, and strange satyrs, minotaurs, and birdlike creatures; and Susanna Coffey, who uses herself as her subject matter. The gallery also carries many contemporary Russian artists.

**Martha Schneider**, 230 W. Superior St., is a gallery devoted entirely to photography. A gallery owner with an unerringly good eye, Schneider chooses artists who create edgy images, pictures that tell a story. When she started out in the gallery business, she represented outstanding ceramic artists. She still carries some of their work in the back room—you can see it if you ask. She represents a wide variety of artists, including the German photographer Thomas Kellner, who deconstructs famous buildings in his photographs. Cubistic Chen Nong is a contemporary Chinese photographer who creates panoramic Chinese scenes that bring to mind Chinese scrolls. She often delicately hand-colors her prints.

**Zolla-Lieberman Gallery** at 325 W. Huron St. features a wide variety of artists. Deborah Butterfield creates life-size horses from mud, wooden sticks, straw, and scrap metal. Of late she builds the horses and has them cast in bronze. They are majestic, organic creatures that speak of real horses straight from the barn. Butterfield's animals are linear with a lot of *negative space*, but they are complete and seem to breathe. Maria Tomasula's colorful, dramatic, BAROQUE paintings are influenced by Mexican art. Her subject is still life, but it is unlike any other still life that you have seen (for example, flowers forming a figure).

▶    If you have time you can try some of the many other galleries in this area that look interesting to you. Free gallery guides may be found in most of the art showrooms. Otherwise head to the West Loop area for another district of unique art galleries.

Another popular section for art galleries is in Chicago's West Loop. If you are traveling by car, you should be able to find parking, either in a lot or on the street. For public transportation, walk two blocks south on Wells St. to Grand Ave., and take the Grand/Morgan bus going west.

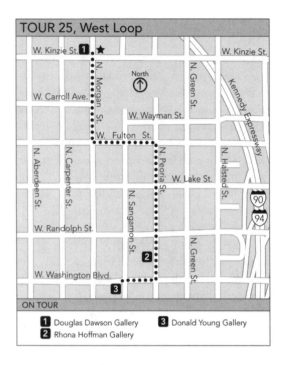

Start at the **Douglas Dawson Gallery** at 400 N. Morgan St. Dawson exhibits non-Western textiles, sculpture, ceramics, and furniture. African, Asian, and pre-Columbian art share space in a fascinating gallery.

The **Rhona Hoffman Gallery** at 118 N. Peoria St. carries the work of long-established as well as emerging artists, including Vito Acconci (see p. 203), Sol LeWitt (see pp. 95, 183–184), Jenny Holzer, Judy Ledgerwood (see pp. 206–207), and Chris Garofalo. Garofalo creates three-dimensional, organic creatures that make you wonder where this form of life comes from. Some of his varied textures and added on forms look lethal but, though threatening, are always beautiful and seductive.

The **Donald Young Gallery**, 933 W. Washington Blvd., also represents CONTEMPORARY artists, including Martin Puryear (see pp. 187–188) Puryear's one-man show at the gallery in 2005 was spectacular. Young also represents Sol Le-Witt (see pp. 95, 183–184) and Bruce Nauman (see p. 187). Anne Chu does painted sculptures using wood, papier-mâché, or pottery. Her work is influenced by ancient CHINESE ART, such as work from the TANG DYNASTY and Western MEDIEVAL design. She reinvents the old, giving it a more casual demeanor. Rebecca Warren redoes the sculpture of Degas and Rodin with a cavalier disregard for tradition.

▶   You may wish to visit other galleries if you have more time. If you are hungry, you'll find many restaurants to choose from in a burgeoning neighborhood. One of the most fun is the Wishbone at 1001 W. Washington Blvd., which serves excellent American food with a Southern accent.

To return to the Loop, take the #56 Milwaukee or the #20 Madison bus east.

# Other Sites to See In and Around Chicago

Chicago is such a large city that it's difficult to see everything. This book's tours were chosen to fit within prescribed time boundaries. Some of the city's art and architecture could not be conveniently seen in any of the hour-long tours. Here are some other highlights of Chicago and areas not previously covered that you may wish to explore.

**McCormick Place** at 2301 S. Lake Shore Dr. is the huge convention building on the lakefront. The original McCormick Place burned down in 1967; the current Miesian-type building, with a trussed roof and recessed glass walls, was built in 1971 by C. F. Murphy Associates. It is enormous but built low so as not to compete with the lake. The simple, well-proportioned building covers 19 acres and is pleasing to look at. Inside, the visitor may become disoriented and confused because of the overwhelmingly large and less-than-humanistic space. A second building, **McCormick Place North,** was added to the complex in 1986 to accommodate growing convention business. This gargantuan structure looms over cars headed south on S. Lake Shore Dr. It was designed by Skidmore, Owings and Merrill and is not as visually successful as its partner on the lake. **McCormick Place South**, built by Thompson, Ventulett, Stainback and Associates in 1996, is more graceful and has won many awards.

A stadium within a stadium—the new Soldier Field.

**McCormick Place West**, designed by the same firm and built in 2007, is more pleasing to the eye. A tunnel will recycle rainwater from the roof of the building into Lake Michigan. It is gigantic, built of glass and concrete, but in spite of its great size it appears more friendly and welcoming than its relatives.

In this same vicinity is **Soldier Field** at 1410 S. Museum Campus Dr. This GRECO-ROMAN, *Doric*-style, colonnaded stadium was built in 1926 by Holabird and Roche as a monument to the veterans of World War I. In 2003, frustrated in their efforts to tear down the landmark building, the City of Chicago and the Chicago Bears football team (which plays at Soldier Field) commissioned Wood and Zapata with Lohan, Caprile, Goettsch and Associates to build a stadium within the existing stadium. The result is described by some as the "toilet bowl rising from the *columns*"; others see it is a UFO about to take off. However you look at it, the new interior has no relationship to the older exterior or to the beautiful Museum Campus nearby. The National Park Service has revoked Soldier Field's inclusion on the National Historic Landmarks list because of the addition.

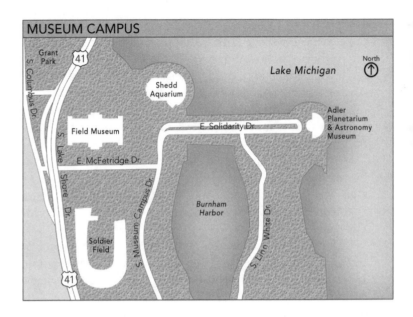

**MUSEUM CAMPUS**

Grant Park
41
Lake Michigan
North ↑
S. Columbus Dr.
Shedd Aquarium
Adler Planetarium & Astronomy Museum
Field Museum
E. Solidarity Dr.
S. Lake Shore Dr.
E. McFetridge Dr.
S. Museum Campus Dr.
Burnham Harbor
S. Linn White Dr.
Soldier Field
41

**Museum Campus** is a lovely parklike campus home to the graceful, NEO-CLASSIC buildings that house three major museums dedicated to the natural sciences: the **Field Museum**, the **Adler Planetarium**, and the **John G. Shedd Aquarium**.

If you are on the Near South Side of the city, you may catch a glimpse of Bertrand Goldberg's **River City** at 800 S. Wells St. You may have noticed these strange, interesting edifices on the river as you moved about the city. The rounded structures are apartment buildings rising from concrete stilts, reminiscent of but different from Goldberg's **Marina City**. These constructions, built between 1964 and 1967, were the first attempt to lure more of Chicago's population south of the Loop. Now, many years after River City was built, the Near South Side has become a favorite site for developers and is heavily dotted with condominiums, apartments, houses, and all the shops and restaurants that inevitably follow in their wake. Other Goldberg buildings that bear a resemblance to River City are Northwestern Memorial's **Prentice Women's**

**Hospital,** 333 E. Superior St. (a newer Prentice is at 250 E. Superior St.), and the **Hilliard Homes** of the Chicago Housing Authority, 2030 S. State St.

If you have an opportunity for a closer look at **Lake Point Tower,** 505 N. Lake Shore Dr. (see pp. 68–70), it is an amazing piece of architecture. It is directly west of that bastion of frantic activity, Navy Pier, but still on the east side of N. Lake Shore Dr.

Just west of Lake Shore Dr. and across from Lake Point Tower, an elegant Santiago Calatrava building that looks like a giant corkscrew is under way. Over 2,000 feet high, about 550 feet taller than Sears Tower, it is another dazzler for Chicago.

The **Vietnam Veterans' Museum** had lost its space at the time of this writing and was searching for a new location. It contained an installation of more than 58,000 dog tags, each imprinted with the name of a soldier killed in the Vietnam War. These tags, the Vietnam War Memorial Wall in Washington, D.C., and a construction by artist Chris Burden, owned by the **Museum of Contemporary Art**, are the only places to make public a complete list of those who died in Vietnam. The idea for the tags came from Ned Broderick and Richard Steinbock; the design was by Mike Helbing and Joe Fornelli. It is an outstanding and significant work of art. Hopefully this excellent small museum will have established itself elsewhere by the time you read this book. You can check its location on the museum's website, www.nvvm.org.

Mies van der Rohe's **860–880 N. Lake Shore Dr.** is a perfect example of his INTERNATIONAL STYLE. These vertical, beautifully proportioned, steel-framed, glass buildings done in 1951 create a rhythm of *piers* and windows that make them transparent sculpture. They are placed on the ground next to—but not even with—each other, creating tension between them. Two companion buildings at **900** and **910 N. Lake Shore Dr.**, designed in 1953 and built in 1956, have a darker glass *curtain wall*. The four buildings standing together are a tribute to MINIMALIST art and architecture. In the 1951 build-

Mies's 860–880 N. Lake Shore Dr. buildings are a tribute to minimalist art and architecture.

ings, Mies composed these beautifully idealized buildings but forgot to include the garbage chutes.

The **Harold Washington Library Center** at 400 S. State St., by architects Hammond, Beeby and Babka, was the winner in an architectural contest sponsored by the City of Chicago to find a new design for the city's main library. The old library, now the **Chicago Cultural Center**, was no longer large enough to accommodate Chicago's growing population. Thomas H. Beeby, who had designed a successful regional library at the intersection of Montrose Ave. and Lincoln Ave. (the **Conrad Sulzer Library**), as well as the beautiful, cohesive Rice addition at the **Art Institute of Chicago**, was chosen. His aggressive, in-your-face structure is red brick and granite with small arches at the base, overwhelmed by the very tall arched windows above. The traditional building is topped with a massive green (weathered copper) *cornice*, sporting gargoyles that are fierce enough to give children nightmares. The north façade with its skin of glass is far more people friendly. The glass is repeated in the *pediments*. A lovely winter garden is at the top of the building.

Louis Sullivan's magnificent **Holy Trinity Russian Orthodox Church**, built in 1903, is at 1121 N. Leavitt St. If you are in that neighborhood, see if the church is open (it is often closed).

At S. Halsted St. and W. Roosevelt Rd., at the edge of the University of Illinois at Chicago campus (just west of the Loop), is a unique art piece called **Skyspace** by James Turrell. A round structure, reminiscent of a halved beehive, it is raised on rectangular stilts and circled by glass just beneath the dome. Inside, viewers sit on benches and look at an elliptical hole in the ceiling where, during the day, the sky appears, becoming a part of the building. It feels a bit like a Magritte painting. From sunset until sunrise, water rains down from the inside top of the stilts, making delicious water sounds that unfortunately don't mask the sound of traffic. As the viewer sits on a bench within the structure, the rain appears to mimic vertical blinds; from outside the structure the water looks like a sheer curtain. The *Skyspace* has enormous potential but doesn't quite work after dark. James Turrell has said of it, "My work is about space and the light that inhabits it. It is about how you confront that space and plumb it. It is about your seeing." The *Skyspace* is always open to the public and free of charge.

If you are on Chicago's North Side, there are many interesting structures to see, including **Graceland Cemetery** at 4001 N. Clark St. The landmark **Getty Tomb** (1890) is one of several designed by Louis Sullivan. An open GREEK temple with two *sarcophaguses* for the **Potter Palmers** was designed by McKim, Mead and White. A lake leading to the tomb by Howard Van Doren Shaw for the **Goodman Family** (of Goodman Theatre fame) became a dramatic approach by boat to the mausoleum for a Goodman son, a playwright who died young. A simple black slab of granite was designed by Dirk Lohan for his grandfather, Mies van der Rohe. This cemetery chronicles the history of Chicago's movers and shakers.

The façade of the old **Krause Music Store** (1922), 4611 N. Lincoln Ave., was the last commission completed by Louis Sullivan before he died. Its recessed door is surrounded by Sullivan's interlaced designs translated into green *terra-cotta*. The building was recently bought by an individual who seems devoted to maintaining the original design.

The **Conrad Sulzer Library** (1985), at Montrose Ave. and Lincoln Ave., is a wonderful building and a welcoming place for people who love books. It was designed by Thomas H. Beeby, who also did the Harold Washington Library (see p. 233).

Farther north is the magnificent **Uptown Theatre**, 4814 N. Broadway, designed by C. W. and George Rapp in 1925. Its BAROQUE ornamentation is unparalleled. As you might notice, this area once was an entertainment center that has fallen into disrepair. The old **Essanay** movie studio nearby at 1345 W. Argyle is where many early movie stars made films. It is an undistinguished, large red brick building now occupied by a Catholic college. An empty space behind the building functioned as the back lot. You can't miss it because the gorgeous, opulent white stone doorway remains. It is topped with a *pediment*, adorned in large letters with the Essanay name. After a day of filming, the executives and actors, such as Charlie Chaplin, would stop at the **Green Mill** at 4802 N. Broadway St. (several doors south of the Uptown Theatre) for a drink. The Green Mill is still there, the oldest bar in Chicago, and has its own interesting history that includes Al Capone. It features great jazz every night and poetry slams on Sunday night.

The **Edgewater Beach Apartments,** at 5555 N. Sheridan Rd., is a pink confection built in 1928 by Benjamin Marshall. Its companion, the now defunct Edgewater Beach Hotel, was also Miami Beach pink with terraces that led all the way to Lake Michigan. The hotel was torn down to make way for an extension of Lake Shore Drive.

The Chicago Architecture Foundation has numerous tours, including a two-hour river trip. For information on reservations and where to board the boat, call 312-922-3432.

While this book is devoted to Chicago proper, the area has many interesting suburbs, among them Evanston and Oak Park. Evanston is just north of the city; for a tour call the Evanston Historical Society at 847-475-3410. The Mary and Leigh Block Art Museum at Northwestern University is certainly worth a visit; call 847-491-4000 for directions to this outstanding gallery. Oak Park is home to a great many Frank Lloyd Wright houses, Wright's Unity Temple, and Wright's home and studio (for a self-guided or guided tour, call 708-848-1976). One of the most beautiful structures in the Chicago area is the Baha'i Temple in the northern suburb of Wilmette. For information, call 847-853-2300.

# An Abbreviated Guide to Architectual Styles and Art History

This short guide briefly explains architectural and art styles most pertinent to an understanding of Chicago architecture and art. (In the text these items appear in SMALL CAPS.) Some of the terms defined as architecture may also be applied to art styles, and are so indicated. When the word "Neo" or "revival" is added to the name of a style, it refers to the adaptation of earlier designs by later cultures.

**Abstract.** Art that does not represent recognizable objects; also referred to as nonobjective or nonfigurative.

**Abstract Expressionism.** Also called Action Painting, it is immediate self-expression without recognizable objects. The artist's innermost thoughts and feelings are the only subject matter. Wassily Kandinsky, a highly religious, introspective, spiritual person, is generally thought of as the first Abstract Expressionist. Kandinsky always wanted to paint with freedom from nature and to make painting more like music.

**Art Deco.** A decorative style that refers to both art and architecture, Art Deco blossomed in the 1920s. It emphasizes verticality and features stylized natural forms translated into geometric shapes. Art Deco objects glorify the machine and give the appearance of being machine-made.

**Barbizon School.** A group of 19th-century landscape painters in the Barbizon region of France who insisted on the truth of what they painted and consequently went outdoors to work.

**Baroque**. A style prevalent especially in the 17th century, marked by complex forms, bold ornamentation, the juxtaposition of contrasting elements, opulence, extravagant theatrical lighting, rich colors, and sweeping curves to indicate movement.

**Bauhaus.** A school opened in Germany in 1919 to train visual artists, architects, craftspeople, and designers in the same basic design principles. The philosophy was to unify art, craft, and technology. The founders believed that unification of the arts and a purified design would bring the highest level of aesthetics to all people. Hitler, fearful of the intellectual thought processes fostered by the school, closed it in the late 1930s. The Bauhaus teachings are applied to art and architecture.

**Beaux Arts.** In French, Beaux Arts means "fine arts." The Beaux Arts combines many styles, starting with a symmetrical, CLASSICAL building that is then adorned with *balustrades*, balconies, *reliefs*, and deep *cornices*. Many of the *reliefs* are BAROQUE in nature.

**Chateau Style.** A 19th-century style influenced by 16th-century French architecture. These buildings have slanting roofs on all sides and vertical dormer windows protruding from the pitched roofs.

**Chicago Imagists.** A group of Chicago artists in the 1960s who broke all the rules of art. Their work, each different in its approach, was nonetheless similar: organic shapes, raw and often vulgar subject matter, and objects influenced by popular images. The Imagists speak of subjects never before mentioned in art nor in polite society. Another similarity in Imagist work is excellent craftsmanship.

**Chinese (Tang Dynasty).** Chinese art is quite similar throughout history. It speaks of organic growth, lack of scientific measurement, dynamic line, and never shows absolute symmetry. There are indications of space but no perspective. In the Tang Dynasty (618–907 A.D.), the artist was influenced by the sensuality of Indian art. Scrolls for painting and landscape painting appeared; pottery became important, its surfaces covered with graceful, rhythmic, vivacious figures.

**Classicism.** Art and architecture based on GRECO-ROMAN ideals.

**Color Field.** Non-OBJECTIVE paintings in which the surface is covered by color. This type of work is based on optical sensations that occur because of the interaction of the colors or tonal *values*.

**Conceptual.** Art in which the idea rather than the finished product is the subject. The artist expresses an experience or the possibility of an experience, and viewers are invited to expand the idea in their minds.

**Constructivism.** Conceived in Russia in the early 20th century, the sculpture of Naum Gabo, Vladimir Tatlin, and Antoine Pevsner was constructed to emphasize negative space rather than solid forms.

**Contemporary.** Art crafted after 1945, including POP, NEW REALISM, and CONCEPTUAL.

**Cubism.** There are two types of Cubism. In **Analytical Cubism** the model is reduced to a geometric form, a cube, and all sides of that figure or object are presented simultaneously. In **Synthetic Cubism** the artist begins with shapes and builds an object or figure from the shapes.

**Dada.** The anti-art statement which declares that people are absurd because they behave so badly toward others, and if they are absurd, all their endeavors, including art, are also absurd. The movement was triggered by the horrors of World War I.

**De Stijl.** The canvas is asymmetrically divided into rectangles, and the *primary colors* plus black and white fill the rectangles. De Stijl attempts to achieve the essence of the perfect underlying composition of the world.

**Deconstructivism.** A radical 20th-entury approach to architecture. The architect pulls apart the forms of a building and rearranges them in new ways. The inner framework is often exposed, and the structures sometimes have a dramatic if disturbing sense of being unstable. These designs are antithetical to INTERNATIONAL STYLE and somewhat akin to the 16th-century style of MANNERISM.

**Divisionism (Pointillism).** Art created by placing dots of color beside each other. The viewer mixes the colors optically.

**Early Christian Art**. When Constantine declared Christianity the official religion of the Roman Empire, the church had to find a way to educate an illiterate population in the tenets of the faith. Pictures were the logical means, but Christianity forbad images that copied acts of God. The solution was to use flat figures with arbitrary proportions and two-dimensional space to symbolize but not mimic the world that God created.

**Earthworks.** The artist manipulates a natural terrain by building up or taking away from the earth. The new form of the land is photographed and presented for viewing. It is a form of CONCEPTUAL art, pertinent in a world concerned with environmental issues.

**Expressionism.** The expression of free, honest emotion. Expressionism is mainly linked to the German Expressionists and the ABSTRACT EXPRESSIONISTS.

**False Images**. See CHICAGO IMAGISTS.

**Fauvism.** The use of brilliant, arbitrary color, flattened images, and many patterns to express the artist's feelings about the subject.

**Flemish.** Paintings done in Flanders in the 15th century (and beyond). The most minute and obsessive of details were painted in rich colors, using a great deal of symbolism.

**Folk Art.** Art produced outside of mainstream artistic styles by untutored artists. The subjects are often about the artist's environment, culture, and religion.

**Georgian.** A balanced, classical style of architecture with a hipped roof.

**Gothic.** Gothic architecture in the 13th and 14th centuries emphasized peaked vertical forms with interlaced, intertwined surface design elements and many windows. The theme of Gothic design seems to be "more is better."

**Greco-Roman/Italian Renaissance Architecture.** Greek and Roman architecture and its influence on the Italian Renaissance plays a large part in Chicago's early architectural philosophy. See the individual listings.

**Greek.** Early Greeks sought to express the ideal, using perfect proportions and striving to capture the ultimate beauty that lived in the Greek mind and body, and in all that the Greeks did. Greeks used *columns* to define their architecture; the Greek *columns* were humanistic and had psychological meaning. *Doric columns* were the shortest, heaviest *columns* with the simplest *capital*. Influenced by the proportions of the human form, they allowed people passing a building to measure themselves favorably against the structure without feeling overwhelmed. *Ionic columns* are taller and more slender, with a slightly more elaborate *capital*. They speak of technical prowess and the inner elegance of peo-

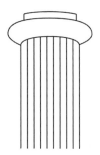

ple. The tallest, most slender *columns*, and the ones best loved by the Romans, had the most elaborate capitals and are called *Corinthian*. As the more slender *columns* taper and rise at the higher levels of the building, they serve to enhance perspective in the viewer's eye.

**Impressionism.** Impressionist art is the observance of natural light and how that light affects form. Brushstrokes are short, shattering solidity and conveying a sense of refracted light as it describes various planes of space. Impressionists went into nature to paint, recording what they actually saw.

**Installation Art.** Artwork created for a particular space, which changes that environment.

**International Style.** The International Style, initiated by Mies van der Rohe at the Bauhaus, is characterized by simple vertical and horizontal lines that expose the elements used in building. There is no applied surface décor. Windows, in bands, cover the surface like a glass curtain. The beautiful relationships of all the elements in the building and the strength of the materials become the décor. This style reveals the essence of what a building is, free of historic connections.

**Islamic Art.** Human images are forbidden by the Koran. Although some flat figures with arbitrary proportions appear in secular work, most Islamic artists develop beautiful ornamental designs, often with stylized motifs from nature. The work features repeated patterns, often intertwined and interlaced. The designs bear a resemblance to calligraphy and are rich in color and form.

**Italian Renaissance.** In the Renaissance, the *columns* of early Rome were replaced with heavy, textured stone at the base, which grounds the building and affords it a scale corresponding to the sturdy build of people (like *Doric columns*). The stone grows smoother, less detailed, and smaller as it moves up and symbolically creates the same humanistic response as the *columns* did. On the outside of both the early RO-MAN Coliseum and the buildings of the Italian Renaissance, floors are articulated so that the building appears to grow rather than looming upward like a threatening giant. Greco-Roman and Renaissance Revival movements were (and remain) popular in Chicago. In art the ideal is emphasized.

**L'art Brut.** Raw art that speaks of the primitive and the deepest expression from within the artist.

**Mannerism.** Mannerist work is ABSTRACT in concept and anxious in demeanor, and the space is overcrowded and ambiguous. Everything is exaggerated and artificial, and features arbitrarily proportioned, often impossibly elongated, boneless bodies. Earlier, ITALIAN RENAISSANCE art (15th to mid-16th century) had been concerned with order, logic, naturalism, coolness, self-containment, humanism, perfection of human proportion, and mathematically accurate space. Beginning in the mid-16th century, the RENAISSANCE world grew agitated over political and economic problems as well as corruption in church and state. Young artists, responding to social tumult, banded together under the label of mannerism (mannered, non-natural art), sending an anti-Renaissance message.

**Medieval Art.** The period of art from the 5th to the end of the 14th century remained under the influence of early Christian art, which did not allow artists to copy what only God was meant to do. Space was flattened, and arbitrarily proportioned figures were used as symbols. Medieval times were less depressed than the early Christian era, and so brighter colors, the incorporation of gold, and elaborate designs were widely used with the unnatural figures.

**Minimal Art.** A movement of 20th-century painters that pares paintings and sculpture to the essence of the artistic message. This style is beyond ABSTRACTION, stripping away everything but the bare—often (but not always) geometric—essentials of composition. In order to understand and appreciate minimalist painting, the viewer must spend time observing the subtle tonal *values*, brushstrokes, proportions, and colors to understand how the elements relate to one another.

**Modernism.** Art, architecture, and design from the beginning of the 20th century until 1945. Experiments in art, moving away from the traditional, actually began in the 19th century with the onset of the Industrial Revolution and the American and French revolutions. Twentieth-century artists, facing even more momentous change, became enchanted with science and technology, and were drawn to a connection with nature that the tribal artists had pursued. The result of modern thinking and questioning resulted in such styles as CUBISM, FAUVISM, ABSTRACTION, DADA, SURREALISM, and DE STIJL.

**Monster Roster.** A combination of EXPRESSIONIST and SURREAL art done by a group of Chicago artists in the 1940s and 1950s. Influenced by L'ART BRUT.

**New Realism.** Reacting against ABSTRACTION, artists began to create art in a super-naturalistic manner. The work was often done by projecting an enlarged photograph onto a surface and copying it, or by placing a grid onto a photograph and a corresponding grid onto canvas or paper, then exactly copying the photo.

**Objective Art.** Art with natural objects or figures.

**Palladian Architecture.** Palladio was a 16th-century architect who designed logical, symmetrical villas, churches, and other buildings. His balanced work sometimes referred to asymmetrical, slightly off-balance MANNERIST elements. Palladian windows are topped by rounded arches or triangular *pediments*.

**Performance Art.** An arranged performance before a live audience, which replaces painting or sculpture. Aspects of some of the performances might not be allowed in a traditional theater.

**Pointillism.** See DIVISIONISM.

**Pop.** The imagery used in this art is borrowed from popular culture and advertising. It was a reaction against ABSTRACT art, thought by some to be too intellectual and highbrow.

**Post-Impressionism.** Some artists who were influenced by IMPRESSIONISM moved away from that style to explore and express individual artistic interests. (See Tour 18 of the Art Institute's 19th-century artwork.)

**Postmodernism.** Postmodern buildings use historical references in contemporary buildings, often referring to more than one style in the same structure. Sometimes there is a harmonious blending of the technological new and the historic old, but the juxtaposition doesn't always work.

**Prairie Style.** Frank Lloyd Wright passionately believed that the lines of buildings should follow the lines of the landscape. He worked in the Midwest where the landscape was flat. Prairie designs usually have deep *cornices* protecting the interior from sun and wind. Prairie Style was also influenced by Japanese architecture.

**Pre-Raphaelite.** An art movement of the mid-19th century in which the Pre-Raphaelite Brotherhood attempted to revive the religious subject matter and excellent craftsmanship of MEDIEVAL art.

**Primitive.** The art of non-Western or prehistoric cultures. The connotation of the word is often misleading: the concept and design of so-called primitive work is usually a sophisticated cultural expression.

**Queen Anne Style.** An architectural style popular in the late 19th century, Queen Anne Style features asymmetrical houses with steep, pitched roofs and lavish decorations, such as fancy posts, spindles, and turrets. If a little bit was good, a lot was much better.

**Rococo.** An ornate 18th-century French style with an emphasis on curvilinear forms, ROMANTIC themes, and pastel colors. It can also refer to curvilinear, overly decorated architecture.

**Roman.** Roman styles were influenced by GREEK architecture, but with important differences. The Romans wished to exhibit physical strength and worldwide power through their buildings, arches, and commemorative *columns* while still expressing concern for the individual by using humanistic proportions. Thus they copied the Greeks but tempered the GREEK style to express power. The Romans used all three GREEK style *columns* in the Coliseum.

**Romanesque.** Medieval churches are Romanesque, built in the Latin cross design. Barrel, or rounded, arches made it possible to reach greater heights. Very heavy walls with few windows contain the outward pressure asserted by the arches.

**Romantic.** Art in which the emotions, imagination, and mystery were stressed. This art was a reaction against the classical style of a logical, ordered universe sometimes seen as coldly removed from the emotions of the individual.

**Surrealism.** An external artistic expression of the unconscious mind, the dreams of the artist.

**Symbolism.** Form and color are used to symbolize what the artist feels about the subject matter of the painting or sculpture. It also refers to the use of forms or objects that refer to things other than what they appear to be.

**WPA Art.** The Works Progress Administration (WPA) was established in the 1930s by the federal government to provide employment for Americans unable to find work because of the Great Depression. Artists were hired to create public art: sculptures and murals for government buildings, including schools, libraries, post offices, and administrative buildings.

# Glossary of Architecture and Art Terms

(In the text these terms appear in *italics*.)

**ABA.** An architectural abbreviation, symbolizing A = base, B = shaft, A = capital.

**assemblage.** A 20th-century work that has been "assembled" from found objects.

**automatic writing (drawing).** Writing or drawing that does not come from conscious thought. The artist's hand is allowed to wander freely, and the result is stream of consciousness. Important to DADA, SURREALISM, and ABSTRACT EXPRESSIONISM.

**balustrade.** A decorative railing supported by short *columns* called *balusters*.

**barrel vault.** A series of arches made of stone, concrete, or brick. They must be buttressed at the sides where the pressure thrusts outward.

**black-box theater**. A small or medium-size theater.

**bronze casting.** A model is made in wax and then covered in a material that will capture the details of the wax. Several holes are made in the mold, the wax is melted away, and liquid bronze is poured into the holes of the mold. After the liquid hardens, the mold is broken away.

**buttress.** A projecting support for a wall.

**cantilever.** An element of a building that projects beyond the wall, such as a balcony or roof. It is balanced behind the wall.

**cella.** The room atop the *ziggurat* that is used for religious purposes.

**chiaroscuro.** A strong use of shading, dark and light, to give a sense of space.

**Chicago window.** The *Chicago window* consists of three windows in one: a large stationary center window flanked by two narrow windows that can be opened. This design captures a maximum amount of light in a city that is often overcast.

**chromogenic.** A color print made from a color slide.

**coffered ceiling.** Framed, recessed panels creating a pattern that moves the eye in and out of space as the frame comes forward and the panel remains recessed.

**collage.** An artwork made up partially or entirely of materials glued to the surface of paper or canvas.

**column.** A vertical form made up of a base, shaft, and capital. It acts as a support.

**combine.** Same as *assemblage*. Robert Rauschenberg called his work *combines* or *assemblages*.

**complementary colors.** Colors across the color wheel from each other. They have nothing in common and consequently intensify each other, such as red and green, yellow and violet, or orange and blue.

**construction.** Nontraditional sculpture that is fabricated and assembled.

**conventions.** Rules of ancient Egyptian art. (See Tour 15.)

**Corinthian column.** The tallest, most slender of the GREEK columns, it has an elaborate capital formed by several rows of sculpted acanthus leaves.

**cornice.** A projection over a building, usually from the roof.

**cuneiform.** The wedge-shaped alphabet of Mesopotamia.

**curtain wall.** A glass skin covering the frame of a building.

**cylindrical.** Rounded.

**Doric column.** The shortest and heaviest of the GREEK columns. A baseless shaft rises to the simplest of capitals, an unadorned shape often referred to as a pillow.

**encaustic.** Paintings that are made by mixing paint and wax. Heat makes the mixture adhere to the surface.

**entablature.** The horizontal part of the building between the roof and the *columns* (or wall). It contains the *frieze* and the *cornice*.

**etching.** A metal plate is covered with an acid-resistant resin, and lines are etched into the resin to expose the metal beneath. The plate is treated with acid, which eats into the uncovered metal. The lines etched by the acid are printed.

**existential.** A philosophy which declares that we are all free, alone, and responsible for ourselves in a purposeless world.

**fertility figures.** Figures with exaggerated breasts and stomachs to express pregnancy. Made to encourage the gods to create more people.

**floating foundation.** Devised to give stability to a building constructed in wet, sandy soil. Tubular concrete caissons are sunk into the bedrock and *cantilevered* out to meet the walls, creating a foundation that distributes the building's weight and acts as a raft as it moves with the unstable, muddy, shifting earth.

**fluted.** Vertical channels carved into a *column*. The eye moves as it flows in and out of the flutes, giving the heavy *column* a lighter feel.

**flying buttress.** An arched support "flying" from a wall or lower roof to contain the outward pressure of the wall.

**fresco.** A method of painting on wet plaster. The paint is absorbed by the plaster, so the painting becomes one with the wall when it dries.

**frieze.** A band around the top of a wall. It usually has decoration, or a *relief* sculpture, within it.

**Gothic rose window.** In a GOTHIC church, a large, round window filled with stained glass of many colors.

**Gothic tracery.** Organic, decorative designs carved in stone and found around the windows of GOTHIC cathedrals.

**graffiti.** Words or drawings scribbled on public walls.

**hierarchical.** A graded size of figures, with the most important figure being the largest.

**Ionic column.** A tall, slender column whose capital features two coiled forms that look snail-like, one on each side of the capital.

**kitsch.** Art or design that is shallow, pretentious, tasteless, and thoughtless—but derives a sense of cheap charm from these qualities.

**lithograph.** Drawing with a greasy crayon or ink on a stone. Water is applied to the surface and greasy ink is rolled onto the stone. Since oil repels water, only the drawing will accept the ink and print.

**maquette.** A small model of an artist's idea for a sculpture.

**mastaba.** Original burial tombs for Egyptian aristocracy.

**medieval illuminated manuscript.** A hand-printed and drawn manuscript with some symbolic figures but primarily beautiful, ornamental designs. These designs were brilliantly colored, used gold in the painting, and often featured interlaced forms.

**mobile.** A sculpture that actually moves. Usually the work is suspended and is moved by air.

**mosaic.** Artwork created by placing small pieces of glass, ceramic, or marble into cement.

**naive art.** Art created by an untrained artist.

**negative/positive space.** The space formed by both what is drawn, formed, or simply exists (positive) and the air that surrounds it (negative).

**Nike.** A winged figure of victory. The wings are clipped so that victory cannot fly away.

**pediment.** The triangular shape formed by the slant of a roof.

**peristyle.** In a Roman home, an open area, often a garden surrounded by *columns*. At Millennium Park in Chicago, the curved, colonnaded structure symbolically enclosing a small area.

**perspective.** A measured system to create the illusion of a three-dimensional space on a two-dimensional surface.

**photogram.** A photographic print made without a negative. Objects are composed, laid onto light-sensitive photographic paper, and exposed to controlled light. The paper is chemically treated, and the parts of the paper that were covered remain white. If a bit of light filters through the object, there are degrees of grey; the background that was not protected from light is black. When Man Ray invented this method of printing he called the impressions or prints "rayograms."

**pier.** A vertical, architectural support; *column*-like.

**pointed arches.** Arches that come to a point instead of being rounded. The weight is directed downward instead of outward, so that the walls do not have to contain the pressure and can be opened to windows.

**portal arches.** Small, flat moldings, called fillets, used to join columns and girders for bracing.

**primary colors.** Red, yellow, and blue are colors that come from nature and cannot be produced by mixing. If they are mixed with one another, however, they form every color in the world.

**relief.** A sculpture that is not freestanding but projects from and is attached to a fixed background.

**ribbed groined vault.** Slender, *pointed arches*, joined at right angles to form a groin, and forming a supportive framework where pressure points down instead of out. When many arches are bundled together they can support a great deal of weight and still maintain their delicate appearance.

**Roman arches and domes.** In rounded arches and domes, masonry is placed one piece above the other, tapering toward the top. A keystone is placed at the very top to hold both sides together.

**rusticated.** Stone with an unpolished, rough surface.

**sarcophagus.** A coffin.

**setbacks.** Upper sections of a building set back to form a section that is reminiscent of steps. This design gives a lighter look to large buildings and also allows light into more windows of the building.

**silk screen.** A method of printing in which a design is laid onto a frame covered with silk or nylon. The areas that are not to be printed are then coated with an impenetrable material. Ink is then dragged from the top to the bottom of the screen. To print other colors, the screen is cleaned and the coating reapplied to other areas, and the printing is repeated.

**skeletal construction.** The use of a metal framework, a lightweight skeleton to support a building.

**slip.** Clay thinned to a creamy consistency and used as glue or as a coating on pottery.

**spandrel.** Triangular space between arches.

**Spanish foil.** A simple, dark background that makes the figure or object of a painting stand out. It also flattens the image. Used widely by Spanish artists in the 17th century.

**stabile.** A stationary sculpture that gives a sense of great movement because of its sweeping composition.

**stele.** An upright slab of stone, clay, or metal with a design, an inscription. It is generally used as a monument.

**terra-cotta.** Clay of a reddish-brown color.

**tone.** Light and dark shades.

**trompe l'oeil.** French for "fool the eye." Painting made to look so real that objects seem to be three dimensional, existing in the real world.

**value.** Lightness and darkness.

**weight-bearing.** A means of building brick or stone upon brick or stone, with each line bearing the weight of what is above it.

**woodblock print.** The artist, using a block of wood, carves away the parts that should not print. Ink is rolled onto the surface, and what hasn't been cut away makes a mark.

**ziggurat.** A Mesopotamian temple that consisted of a man-made mountain with ramps for ascending and descending. The mountain was topped by a *cella*, a room for worship.

**zone.** In Egypt, a rectangular band measured onto a surface (usually the wall of a tomb). The artist organized and portrayed a story in the zone or zones to ensure that the story was told in an orderly fashion. This device was also borrowed for use in Mesopotamia, for paintings on Greek vases, woven into tapestries during medieval times, and most familiarly, is now used in modern comic strips.

# Photo Credits

ARCHITECTURE

All photographs © Ron Gordon, with the following exceptions:

Second Presbyterian Church's Tiffany Window (p. 11), Martin Cheung, courtesy of Friends of Historic Second Church.

Carson Pirie Scott building (p. 37), Joseph Freed and Associates LLC.

Millennium Park (p. 47), City of Chicago / Peter J. Schulz.

Roosevelt University (p. 55), Roosevelt University / Prakarn Nisarat.

Illinois Institute of Technology images (pp. 218, 219, 220) courtesy of the Illinois Institute of Technology, Richard Barnes.

Soldier Field (p. 230), Brook Collins / Chicago Park District.


ARTWORKS

Agora courtesy of Jaime Darang.

Images from the Oriental Institute courtesy of the Oriental Institute of the University of Chicago.

Domenico Theotokópoulos, called El Greco, Spanish, b. Greece, 1541–1614, The Assumption of the Virgin, 1577–79, Oil on canvas, 158-3/4 x 83-3/4 in. (403.2 x 211.8 cm), Gift of Nancy Atwood Sprague in memory of Albert Arnold Sprague, 1906.99 unframed. Reproduction, The Art Institute of Chicago.

Rembrandt Harmenszoon van Rijn, Dutch, 1606–1669, Old Man with a Gold Chain, c.1631, Oil on panel, 32-3/4 x 29-3/4 in. (83.1 x 75.7 cm), Mr. and Mrs. W. W. Kimball Collection, 1922.4467 Photograph by Bob Hashimoto. Reproduction, The Art Institute of Chicago.

Giovanni Battista Tiepolo, Italian , 1696–1770, Rinaldo Enchanted by Armida, 1742/45, Oil on canvas, 73-13/16 x 85-3/8 in. (187.5 x 216.8 cm), Bequest of James Deering, 1925.700 Reproduction, The Art Institute of Chicago.

Eugène Delacroix, French, 1798–1863, Lion Hunt, 1860/61, Oil on canvas, 76.5 x 98.5 cm, Potter Palmer Collection, 1922.404 Reproduction, The Art Institute of Chicago.

Edouard Manet, French, 1832–1883, Beggar with a Duffle Coat (Philosopher), 1865, Oil on canvas, 73-7/8 x 43-1/4 in. (187.7 x 109.9 cm), A. A. Munger Collection, 1910.304 Reproduction, The Art Institute of Chicago.

Pierre-Auguste Renoir, French, 1841–1919, Two Sisters (On the Terrace), 1881, Oil on canvas, 100.5 x 81 cm, Mr. and Mrs. Lewis Larned Coburn Memorial Collection, 1933.455 Reproduction, The Art Institute of Chicago.

Claude Monet, French, 1840–1926, Stacks of Wheat (Sunset, Snow Effect), 1890–91, Oil on canvas, 25-11/16 x 39-1/2 in. (65.3 x 100.4 cm), Potter Palmer Collection, 1922.431 Reproduction, The Art Institute of Chicago.

Georges Seurat, French, 1859–1891, A Sunday on La Grande Jatte, 1884, 1884–86, Oil on canvas, 81-3/4 x 121-1/4 in. (207.5 x 308.1 cm), Helen Birch Bartlett Memorial Collection, 1926.224 combination of quadrant captures F1, F2, G1, G2. Reproduction, The Art Institute of Chicago.

Hilaire Germain Edgar Degas, French, 1834–1917, The Millinery Shop, 1884–90, Oil on canvas, 100 x 110.7 cm, Mr. and Mrs. Lewis Larned Coburn Memorial Collection, 1933.428 Pre-Treatment. Reproduction, The Art Institute of Chicago.

Vincent van Gogh, Dutch, 1853–1890, The Bedroom, 1889, Oil on canvas, 73.6 x 92.3 cm, Helen Birch Bartlett Memorial Collection, 1926.417 Reproduction, The Art Institute of Chicago.

Henri de Toulouse-Lautrec, French, 1864–1901, At the Moulin Rouge, 1892/95, Oil on canvas, 48-7/16 x 55-1/2 in. (123 x 141 cm), Helen Birch Bartlett Memorial Collection, 1928.610 Reproduction, The Art Institute of Chicago.

Paul Gauguin, French, 1848–1903, Day of the God (Mahana no Atua), 1894, Oil on canvas, 68.3 x 91.5 cm, Helen Birch Bartlett Memorial Collection, 1926.198 Reproduction, The Art Institute of Chicago.

Paul Cézanne, French, 1839–1906, The Basket of Apples, c.1893, Oil on canvas, 25-7/16 x 31-1/2 in. (65 x 80 cm), Helen Birch Bartlett Memorial Collection, 1926.252 Reproduction, The Art Institute of Chicago.

Pablo Picasso, Spanish, 1881–1973, Daniel-Henry Kahnweiler, 1910, Oil on canvas, 101.1 x 73.3 cm, Gift of Mrs. Gilbert W. Chapman in memory of Charles B. Goodspeed, 1948.561 Reproduction, The Art Institute of Chicago.

Henri Matisse, French, 1869–1954, Interior at Nice, 1919 or 1920, Oil on canvas, 52 x 35 in. (132.1 x 88.9 cm), Gift of Mrs. Gilbert W. Chapman, 1956.339 Reproduction, The Art Institute of Chicago.

Wassily Kandinsky, French, b. Russia; 1866–1944, Painting with Green Center, 1913, Oil on canvas, 43-1/4 x 47-1/2 in. (108.9 x 118.4 cm), Arthur Jerome Eddy Memorial Collection, 1931.510 Reproduction, The Art Institute of Chicago.

Marc Chagall, French, born Vitebsk, Russia (present-day Belarus), 1887–1985, American Windows, 1977, Stained glass, 244 x 978 cm (overall), A gift of Marc Chagall, the City of Chicago, and the Auxiliary Board of The Art Institute of Chicago, commemorating the American Bicentennial in memory of Mayor Richard J. Daley, 1977.938, The Art Institute of Chicago.

Piet Mondrian (Pieter Cornelis Mondriaan), Dutch, 1872–1944, Composition (No.1) Gray-Red, 1935, Oil on canvas, 22-5/8 x 21-7/8 in. (57.5 x 55.6 cm), Gift of Mrs. Gilbert W. Chapman, 1949.518 Reproduction, The Art Institute of Chicago.

Constantin Brancusi, French, born Romania, 1876–1957, Golden Bird, 1919/20 (pedestal c. 1922), Bronze, stone and wood, 85-3/4 in. (with base) h., Partial gift of the Arts Club of Chicago; restricted gift of various donors; through prior bequest of Arthur Rubloff; through prior restricted gift of William Hartmann; through prior gifts of Mr. and Mrs. Carter H. Harrison, Mr. and Mrs. Arnold H. Maremont through the Kate Maremont Foundation, Woodruff J. Parker, Mrs. Clive Runnells, Mr. and Mrs. Martin A. Ryerson, and various donors, 1990.88, The Art Institute of Chicago.

Jackson Pollock, American, 1912–1956, Greyed Rainbow, 1953, Oil on canvas, 182.9 x 244.5 cm, Gift of Society for Contemporary American Art, 1955.494 Reproduction, The Art Institute of Chicago.

Gerhard Richter, German, born 1932, Woman Descending the Staircase, 1965, Oil on canvas, 79 x 51 in. (200.7 x 129.5 cm), Roy J. and Frances R. Friedman Endowment; gift of Lannan Foundation, 1997.176 Reproduction, The Art Institute of Chicago.

Sol LeWitt, American, b. 1928, Nine Part Modular Cube, 1977, Baked enamel on aluminum, 219.7 x 219.7 x 219.7 cm, Ada Turnbull Hertle Fund, 1978.1022 Reproduction, The Art Institute of Chicago.

Eva Hesse, American, b. Germany, 1936–1970, Hang-Up, 1966, Acrylic on cord and cloth, wood, and steel, 182.9 x 213.4 x 198.1 cm, Through prior gifts of Arthur Keating and Mr. and Mrs. Edward Morris, 1988.130 Reproduction, The Art Institute of Chicago.

Jim Nutt, American, b. 1938, Miss E. Knows, 1967, Acrylic on Plexiglas, aluminum, rubber, enamel on wood frame, 192.1 x 131.1 cm (75-5/8 x 51-5/8 in.), Twentieth-Century Purchase Fund, 1970.1014 Recto. Photograph by Robert Hashimoto. Reproduction, The Art Institute of Chicago.

Ed Paschke, American, 1939–2004, Minnie, 1974, Oil on canvas, 50-3/8 x 38 in., Gift of the Robert A. Lewis Fund in memory of William and Polly Levey, 1982.397 Reproduction, The Art Institute of Chicago.

Kerry James Marshall, OneTrue Thing, Meditations on Black Aesthetics, Collection Museum of Contemporary Art, Chicago; Bernice and Kenneth Newberger Fund. Photography © Museum of Contemporary Art, Chicago.

Alejandro García Nelo, Retablo, 2000, Mixed Media, Courtesy of the National Museum of Mexican Art, Photo by Dionicio Ontiveros.

# Index

## A NOTE ON THE AUTHOR

Ann Slavick, an art educator, is also a painter and sculptor. She has led tours of Chicago art and architecture for students as well as professional organizations. A resident of Chicago, she holds a BFA and a masters in Art History, Theory, and Criticism from the School of the Art Institute of Chicago.

917.731104 CHI

JUL 2 3 2008

Slavick, Ann.

Hour Chicago : twenty-five
self-guided 60-minute tours
of Chicago's great
architecture and art